The Hikers Guide to O'ahu

Mauka Trails of Hawai'i

John Alford

'Ohana Publishing

The Mountain Biker's Guide to Oʻahu
Mauka Trails of Hawaiʻi
December 1995

All rights reserved
Copyright © 1995 John Alford

Written by John Alford
Edited by John Clark
Production (Macintosh/Quark XPress®) by Blair Thorndike
Maps (Macintosh/Adobe Illustrator®) by Alec White
Illustrations by Curt Evans
Front cover photo from Manoa Cliff Trail and back cover photo from the Old Pali Road Trail by Morgan Blank

No part of this book may be reproduced or transmitted in any form or by any means, electrical or mechanical, including photocopying, recording, or by any information storage and retrieval system, without permission in writing from the publisher, except for the inclusion of brief quotations in a review.

For information, contact:
ʻOhana Publishing
P.O. Box 240170
Honolulu, HI. 96824-0170
email: mtnbike@aloha.net

Library of Congress Catalog Card Number 95-92844
ISBN 0-9649843-0-X
Product of Hawaiʻi

Acknowledgements

From the Heart

First of all, I want to thank my dear friends and family who helped to make this book possible. Your help with this book has been most appreciated.

Mahalo to computer specialists Alec White for the map designs and Blair Thorndike for production. Also, a sincere mahalo to John Clark for editing.

Special thanks are due to my riding partners, Preston Maginis, Mike Weisbrod, Ed McConville, Chris Petterson, Ken Mackie, Paul Aurely and Latigo Biggins. You have patience beyond the word. To my hiking partners and true friends Chrysoula Coletsis, John Connors, Shar Sylva and Kristy Maharrey. Thanks for waiting for me. Thanks to Keith "Picture Man" Herron, Martin Robinson and Twain Newhart for the few fabulous photos. Many thanks to Morgan Blank for the Mac-powerbook loaner in a time of need and for the cover shots. Mahalo to Curt Evans of Down/Up for the illustrations. Special thanks to Department of Land and Natural Resources, Division of Forestry and Wildlife, Curt Cottrell, Aaron Lowe and Jim Spruil of Na Ala Hele, and Betsy Gagne and Randy Kennedy of the Natural Area Reserves Commission for your valuable time and wealth of information.

Mahalo to my employer, Mercy Ambulance, who most graciously accepted my attention to this project. Thanks to Wally Parcels of the Bikefactory Sportshop for your encouragement, generosity and contributions. Thank you to Ronnie Tysie of the Pacific Business Center for your support. Thanks to Kim Gennaula of KGMB TV for your help.

To my mother and father, bless you both for teaching me to love the land and respect mother earth. To my brothers Kenny and Tommy and my sister, Nancy, thank you for your encouragement.

Finally, I thank God for granting me the fortitude to complete this project. I have dreamed of writing a book about mountain biking, and as an outdoor enthusiast, I believe this guide fulfills my dream and says what needs to be said.

And last of all, my Rocky Mountain cycle. Thanks for the ride! Mahalo to all, from the heart.

Contents

Acknowledgements..iii
Introduction...vi
Interpretation of information..iix

1 Mountain Biking Hawai'i.
Trail access - public, private or endangered............................10

2 The Environment.
Hawaiian weather..13
Wildlife and insects...15
Hawai'i's Flora...17

3 Trail Preservation
Education..20
Proper riding techniques..23
Get involved in trail maintenance..25

4 Mountain Biking Safety
Hazards...28
Mountain biking safety tips..30
Safety accessories..32
Before you ride..33

5 Bicycle Maintenance
Maintaining your mountain bike...34
Cleaning your bike...36

6 Hawai'i's Competition Scene
Then and now..38

O'ahu Map..42
Legend..43

Ko'olau Range Trail Maps
Makapu'u Lighthouse Road - East O'ahu (wet ride ok)..............45
Kuli'ou'ou - Southeast O'ahu..49
Wiliwilinui Ridge - South O'ahu (wet ride ok)...........................51
Wa'ahila - South O'ahu..55
Tantalus - South O'ahu (Endangered) map not included............57
'Aiea Loop - Central O'ahu..59
Manana - Central O'ahu..61
West Kaunala - North O'ahu...65
Hau'ula Loop - Northeast O'ahu..67
Ma'akua Ridge - Northeast O'ahu..71
Maunawili (map A) - East O'ahu..73
Maunawili (map B) - East O'ahu..75

Wai'anae Range Trail Maps
Kuaokala F.R. via KPSTS - West O'ahu (wet ride ok)................79
Mokule'ia Access Road to Peacock Flats - Northwest O'ahu (wet ride ok)........81
Kealia - Northwest O'ahu..83
Ka'ena Point - West O'ahu (wet ride ok)..................................87

7 Private Lands
Mililani - Central O'ahu (wet ride ok).......................................90
Kahuku - North O'ahu (wet ride ok)...91
Queen's Beach - East O'ahu (wet ride ok)................................92

8 Guided Tours
Kualoa Ranch/Ka'a'awa Valley - Northeast O'ahu (wet ride ok)......94
Waimea Valley - North O'ahu (wet ride ok).............................97

Appendix
Permit Information..100
Private Property Access, Bike Tours, Bike Shops.....................101
Bike Rentals, Bike Clubs and Organizations.............................103
Accommodations & Food..106
References..107
Glossary...107
About the Author..110

Introduction

Aloha! Born and raised in Hawai'i, I've seen many changes. One thing that has kept its natural beauty is the pure, awesome and unique mountains of our tropical paradise. It's so easy to speak of the wonders of my home. I

have always enjoyed sharing my mountain biking adventures with others. Now, with the use of this guide, you can see for yourself what it means to ride in Hawai'i.

From the salt sprayed sea cliffs and blue ocean views at Ka'ena Point to the misty green jungles of the Ko'olau Range, this guide will take you on off-road journeys that will bring you back to the days of old Hawai'i. Explore the vast terrain and discover valleys of wild birds and lands of enchantment.

Mauka Trails of Hawai'i is a guide like no other. Choose from arduous uphill fire roads to downhill single tracks. Riders can select appropriate trails to match their individual skill levels, simply by reading the text with each map. Also included are points of interest, terrain changes, a mileage counter, difficult sections and some information on local flora and fauna.

Have fun and please be careful and courteous of other trail users while you enjoy the splendor of our island wonderland. When mountain biking our islands, stop on occasion to take in the views of our tropical landscape and don't forget your camera. These trails are all picture perfect.

The concept of *Mauka Trails of Hawai'i*

I decided to write about O'ahu's mountain biking trails during the spring of 1995. I felt that a book on mountain biking with detailed maps to our unique back country would be the perfect avenue to promote the more important issues such as trail preservation and trail etiquette. This is the vital link to continued mountain biking trail access. Mountain biking has become increasingly popular here in Hawai'i, and it is time that all of us who ride on the public trails recognize that it is a privilege.

All of our mauka trails are unique in every way and deserve your utmost respect and consideration. We need to educate other trail users, as well as the abusers, so that restrictions will not be placed against mountain biking on Hawaiian trails. I hope that with the information contained in this book, we can all work together to be a part of the solution and not the problem. It is the true "Aloha Spirit" that has inspired me to share this information with you, my fellow off-road enthusiasts. Together we can all create a world of shared trail use that works.

Interpretation of information

The information in this guide is my interpretation of the listed trails' terrain, environment and accessibility. The distances of the trails were calculated from a CatEye Vectra bicycle odometer calibrated to a 26-inch wheel. However, allow room for errors. The mileages shown on the maps are estimates and should not be considered as accurate. It is your responsibility to use your own judgement and common sense when riding on these trails.

The following trail ratings are designed to help you select trails that match your riding ability. Riders are expected to meet these minimum requirements when choosing a prospective ride.

Beginner Riders:

Persons who have general knowledge of bicycling. Before going off road, they should be competent in basic skills such as balancing well, stopping, starting, turning, shifting and braking. Beginners must expect bumpy and uneven terrain as common ground for mountain biking.

Intermediate Riders:

Persons who have experience riding on 4-wheel drive roads and narrow single track. They should be competent in skills such as, balancing well on steep uphill and downhill starts and stops, and be able to negotiate a variety of difficult and technical terrain.

Advanced Riders:

Persons who have exceptional judgement, balance and coordination on a bike. Riders are expected to be competent in technical riding skills such as, bunny hopping, doing drop-offs, wheeling and negotiating well over very difficult and technical terrain.

Special note to mountain bikers: DO NOT venture off trails or make your own short cuts. Mountain biking the trails of Hawai'i is a unique privilege and requires your utmost respect. Skidding your rear wheel is very destructive to the trail and should be avoided as much as possible. Do your part to preserve and protect our natural environment and exercise proper riding techniques to minimize impact. The following trails are also used for hiking, and riders should be courteous to other trail users. Be cautious of recreational vehicles and never spook animals. Do not ride at excessive speeds when visibility is poor and stay off single track when it's wet or raining. Help ensure that our trails are kept open to all users and educate your fellow riders in regard to trail preservation and etiquette.

Warning: This guide is strictly informational. It is intended to show you where to gain trail access, and to give you an idea of what to expect. However, because of weather and erosion, the trail conditions may change and exceed your riding abilities. Use these trails at your own risk and always wear protective gear when bicycling.

1 Mountain Biking Hawai'i

Imagine being high on top of the green lush mountains of a tropical island. The misty clouds hug the summit as the songs of wild birds are heard in the blossoming 'ohi'a lehua trees. Deep in the valleys, blankets of rain dampen the earth as waterfalls pour into pools below. The smell of fresh yellow ginger blossoms and over-ripe guava fruit fills the air. As you descend a narrow, winding switchback, you embrace beams of sunlight as they dance through the hapu'u forest around you. This is Mauka Trails of Hawai'i.

Meanwhile, along the coast below, the sunny skies light up the pristine blue Pacific as the cool ocean trade winds blow. The salt sprayed sea cliffs stand tall and dark against the white splash, as powerful Pacific swells pound the rough lava shoreline. Beautiful tropic birds fly high above the sea, looking for today's fresh catch. Awe-struck by the surrounding beauty, sometimes you find it difficult to stay on the trail. Just off-shore, green sea turtles surface for a fresh breath of life before returning to the depths. Further out in the deep blue, a large black shape catches your eye, so you stop to see what it is. Then the mighty tail of a Hawaiian Humpback whale breaches the surface and with a fierce blow, slaps the ocean creating a huge splash, big enough to be seen for miles. You taste the salt in the air and feeling the warmth of the sun, you say to yourself, "this is Mauka Trails of Hawai'i."

Trail access — public, private or endangered

Mountain biking in Hawai'i is a transcendental experience. From mauka to makai (mountains to the sea), the tropical islands of Hawai'i offer the kind of terrain and beauty that all levels of riders can enjoy.

Here in the islands, a variety of public state land is open to hikers and mountain bikers alike, without the need for a permit. All of the these trails were designed for hiking, and mountain bikers should expect to see backpackers, day-hikers and families with small children on the trails. The state's trail system is comprised mostly of single track, or narrow paths cut through raw vegetation. With these trails open to shared use, a few of them are seeing evidence of overuse. The chapter on trail preservation explores several ways to help keep impact at a bare minimum when riding our precious trails.

Some private land owners allow recreational access on their property, but usually by special permission only. Certain landowners or lessees charge a fee, while others may require insurance and indemnification by having you sign a release. Knowing where you are riding and if access is permitted is good sound advice, whether it be Hawai'i or elsewhere. Trespassing is illegal and prosecution may be by government or by the owner.

This guide will introduce you to the trails that are accessible. If permits are necessary, the individual map descriptions will tell you how to go about obtaining them. Calling ahead is recommended to ensure permits are still available. Check Permit Information at the back of the book for local phone numbers.

Some trails included in this guide will be listed as "Endangered". This means that the trail is suffering from overuse and riding restrictions may soon be enacted, if not already. If possible, alternate riding trails should be used. Plans to temporarily close and repair endangered trails are under consideration. Future partial or total trail closures to mountain bikes are not just rumors. Similar restrictions have already occurred in many mainland states in recent years. Aggressive riding styles should be saved for races and 4WD roads, not for precious single tracks. Get educated on our current situation and help protect what we still have. Always observe trail signs and respect the 'aina (land).

Some of the road rides between trail destinations are feasible, but sometimes not practical. The State Department of Transportation has put some effort to improving our roadways and creating more bicycle lanes, but the riding conditions of our highways are still poor. Be very careful when riding the highways of Hawai'i. If the distance between you and the trail is long, drive a car to the trail head. Check the O'ahu Map included in this guide to estimate the distance

When you park a car at the trail head, be sure to obey parking signs. Park on public streets and not in private driveways. Keep your vehicle locked and don't leave valuables in the car which might provoke thieves. If you notice a lot of broken glass on the ground, it would be advisable to park somewhere else, perhaps closer to a house. After all, you have a bike, so make use of it and keep your vehicle safe.

2 The Environment

Hawaiian weather

Hawai'i's mild climate attracts visitors from around the globe. The tropical weather of Hawai'i usually calls for sunshine with occasional showers in the windward and mauka regions. During the winter season, the temperature may drop to the low 60's and 70's but, an 85 degree day is not uncommon. On the other hand, don't be fooled by the cozy warmth of the islands. Snow and ice can be found at higher elevations on Maui and Hawai'i during the winter months. A decrease of 2 to 4 degrees for every 1000 foot elevation is a good way to estimate the temperature at higher elevations. It is a good idea to carry some

warm clothes if you are planning a ride to higher elevations.

Hawai'i's rainfall is more prevalent during the months of October to April. Our rains are usually short bursts and seldom last days at a time. The higher elevations and windward sides of our mountain ranges usually see more precipitation. Sometimes, we experience sunshine with a warm gentle rain that cools the heat of the day. This is referred to as "Liquid Sunshine". Keep in mind, if you are to get caught in a rainstorm while biking, the roads and trails will become very slippery. Wet roots and rocks can cause quick unexpected falls.

During heavy rain, be cautious near river beds. Flash flooding can occur, even when the rain doesn't appear to be strong. The summit above may be raining much harder than where you are and a sudden downpour may be all it takes to create powerful changes in stream flow and water levels.

Our normal northeasterly winds are referred to as "trade winds". Usually steady, these winds cool the heat of the day and help rid the island of air pollution. The trade winds are refreshing and enjoyed even more when working up a sweat.

"Kona" weather is uncomfortable and occurs when hot and humid south winds blow. Sometimes these Kona winds carry a volcanic haze from the big island of Hawai'i. Then the horizon will become lost in a haze of gray, and you'll drip with perspiration, even when just relaxing. Kona weather is most common between the months of October and April.

In the absence of trade winds or storms, diurnal heating and cooling of the islands bring light on-shore breezes during the day switching to off-shore breezes during the night.

The most severe weather in the islands is brought on by hurricanes. From the months of June through November, all eyes are on the satellite maps of the pacific, watching storms that may build into full blown hurricanes. Hurricanes bring extremely high storm surges, huge surf and powerful winds.

Thanks to our highly sophisticated weather warning system and our State Civil Defense, we always receive hurricane warning far in advance.

Sunscreen is a must, especially for those of us with "fair skin". A Skin Protection Factor SPF of 30+ is highly recommended. The sun's rays are strongest between 10 a.m. and 2 p.m. If at all possible, try to ride before and after these extreme hours. If it is a cloudy day, still use sunscreen because the penetrating ultra violet rays can still burn your skin. Wear a hat and a shirt and lather up with a good non-greasy, sweat-proof sunblock.

To avoid dehydration, drink plenty of water and carry extra water with you during your ride. Refer to the "Before you ride" section for a good planner.

Wildlife and insects

Here in Hawai'i, a variety of wildlife can be found. Up mauka, the feral pig (pua'a) is one of our more common wild animals. First introduced by early Polynesian voyagers, the pigs' destructive habits have threatened our Hawaiian rainforests for years. Pigs trample plants and eat the ferns and important undergrowth which holds the top soil in place. The wild boars have tusks, and if cornered or frightened may charge at the threat, but it is highly unlikely that you will ever get this close to a wild pig. They are quick to run when they see or hear people.

Wild goats are also destructive. Sometimes heard from a distance, you're likely to see them clinging to steep and dangerous cliffs in the drier regions such as Ka'ena Point.

The mongoose is a small fury animal which looks like a weasel. Sometimes you'll see one running from shrub to shrub as if playing hide and seek. These little critters, often seen as road-kill, have grown in numbers since their introduction some years ago. The mongoose was supposed to help control our rat population. Unfortunately, rats are nocturnal and the mongoose is not. Now, the mongoose is a problem for our birdlife. In particular, they prey on ground nesting birds and their eggs.

Despite the remoteness of our islands, and Department of Agriculture laws, illegal reptiles and other foreign species continue to make there way to Hawai'i. Many are smuggled in by new residents. Others, such as the brown tree snake, sometimes hitch rides in the wheel wells of planes arriving from foreign places. The introduction of foreign species pose a serious threat to native Hawaiian plants and animals.

Along coastal trails, riders must exercise caution in the event that you encounter an endangered species such as the green sea turtle (honu), or the Hawaiian monk seal ('Ilio holo i ka uaua). The Natural Area Reserves System (NARS) protects these and other species such as the Laysan albatross' that nest along coastal trails. The nesting areas sought by the birds usually have low visitor volume and long runways necessary for their take-offs. It is vital that you adhere to the rules of the

NARS where riding bikes is strictly prohibited.

Hawai'i's little critters known to sting and bite include bees, wasps, red ants, centipedes, scorpions, brown recluse spiders, black widow spiders and the pesky mosquito. With the exception of the mosquito, most of the biting or stinging critters are found in the lower, drier regions. Check the ground beneath you before sitting down to avoid getting goosed by one of these pests.

Mosquitoes and fruit gnats are most prevalent in moist and windless areas. A good splash of repellent should help to keep these pests away. Cockroaches live almost everywhere and while not threatening, are a nuisance. Keep food sealed to avoid sharing your meals with uninvited guests.

Some small leeches have been found in the sugar cane flumes. Swimming in these flumes is not recommended, not only because of leeches, but also because of possible fertilizer, pesticide or bacterial contamination in the water.

One of the biggest concerns for mountain bikers is bees. Typically, our trails have fragrant flowers which bees like to snack on. If you are allergic to stings, you should carry your anti-histamine and anaphylactic kit as prescribed by your doctor, just in case.

Hawai'i's Flora

Along our mauka trails, you will encounter many different types of flora. Listed below are just a few of the species commonly seen.

Our official state tree, the kukui (candlenut tree) is commonly found growing in our lush, green valleys. The kukui's distinctive light green foliage can be seen from more than a mile away. Introduced by early Polynesians, the kukui has been used by Hawaiians for hundreds of years. The kukui nut is very oily and burns quite easily. In days of old Hawai'i, the oil was used to light stone lamps, hence the name candlenut. The nuts are sometimes dried, peeled and polished to be strung as leis. Some folks dry roast the nut and use them as a relish with salt and pepper. Do not mistake these nuts for macadamia nuts. The kukui can also be a very powerful laxative.

Kukui, ginger and banana are some of the common flora.

The dry, coastal regions commonly have an abundance of haole koa. This wild bush grows rampant and is considered to be a weed. It is a distant relative of the native koa tree which possesses a beautiful wood grain that is highly prized for wooden furnishings. Native koa is easily spotted along certain trails with its obvious sickle shaped phyllodes (leaf stems).

'Ohi'a is one of the dominant native trees found on our

mountain trails. The ʻohiʻa lehua blossoms come in a variety of colors including red, orange and pale yellow. Legend says, if you pick these flowers, rains will soon follow.

A wide variety of ferns are also found along the trails. The obvious ground cover on most of our trails is the poky and stem laced false staghorn fern (uluhe). If you are wearing shorts and have to blaze through a patch of overgrown uluhe, be prepared for scratches on your legs.

The hapuʻu is a tree fern which grows a fibrous and golden hairy trunk. Fiddleheads are the developing young fronds which look like a monkey's tale when first sprouting. Slowly unfurling into a beautiful arching green frond, the endemic hapuʻu is a photogenic gift of nature. Unfortunately, these beautiful tree ferns get pushed over and their starchy pith is eaten by destructive feral pigs.

A variety of introduced ginger plants are found along trails in wetter areas. The yellow and white ginger are the only ones with fragrant blossoms. Shampoo ginger or ʻawapuhi kuahiwi was introduced by early Polynesians. The soapy juice squeezed from its buds is still used as a shampoo by campers.

A wide variety of edible fruits are found along the trails. The introduced guava and strawberry guava are the most common. Mountain apples, mangoes, bananas, star fruit, lilikoi (passion fruit) and the native ʻohelo berries are also found on certain trails. Never pick and eat unknown fruit. Refer to References to find out more about our native plants and animals.

3 Trail Preservation

Education

It is imperative that we learn how to share the trails. Educating ourselves about factors that contribute to trail erosion is a good start. Learning riding techniques to minimize impacts on the environment will help preserve the resources and promote shared trail access.

The mountain bike community has grown tenfold since its introduction in the early 1980's. Bike technology is changing so rapidly that most models are outdated within a year. The skill levels of some riders have also gone into a higher dimension. Top riders are performing maneuvers and tricks that were only dreamed about 10 years ago. With this advancement in technology and riding, it is time that biking etiquette move forward, too.

Mountain biking the trails of Hawai'i is a unique privilege. We are blessed to be able to ride some of the most beautiful single tracks in the world. This is a joy that only a relative few can experience. To preserve that privilege, we need to care for the natural environment that surrounds us. As a biker, it is your responsibility to learn the techniques to minimize impacts on the trails.

Responsible riding means to think before you act. Single tracks are not the place to be when conditions are wet. The tearing action of a skidding bicycle tire on a wet trail expedites the erosion process.

Certain sections of low-lying trails trap and hold water, making mud holes long after the rains have fallen. Riders should dismount and carry their bikes around these areas. Riding through mud puddles will only make the problem worse.

During wet and rainy weather, select a trail that can handle it. Four wheel drive roads are the only recommended rides on wet days. This book will guide you to these roads that are accessible during wet weather. Single tracks are precious, and riders should stay on the main trail. Don't make short cuts. This kills the vegetation and adds to erosion. Acts of irresponsible riding also promote a negative image for mountain biking and can lead to increased trail maintenance and/or trail closure.

Irresponsible riding can lead to trail closure.

If you see other trail users such as hikers, other bikers or equestrians, greet them and slow or stop to allow for safe passing. Some of the cliff areas are dangerous and a reckless pass can be frightening and hazardous for everyone on the trail.

All mountain bikers should follow the International Mountain Biking Association's (IMBA) six rules of the trail:
1. Ride on open trails only.
2. Leave no trace.
3. Control your bicycle.
4. Always yield trail.
5. Never scare animals.
6. Plan ahead.

Another way of preserving the trail is not to litter. Pack out what you pack in. Show some "Aloha 'Aina" (love of the land). If you come across other people's trash, pick it up and pack it out if you have the extra space. Do not bury your trash. Local mountain critters will dig it up and make a mess of it. If you have to smoke, be extremely cautious near dry forests or grass, and always bring your butts home. Mahalo for your kokua. (Thank you for your help.)

Another way to preserve the environment is to remove "hitch hikers" (foreign seeds from unwanted plants and weeds) from your clothes. Contamination of native forests with foreign seeds from other countries and/or local mountain ranges pose a serious threat to our fragile ecosystems. Do your part and clean the dirt and debris off your socks, shoes and bike before exploring your next trail. This will dramatically decrease the chances of spreading unwanted vegetation.

Given the opportunity to use these trails, you should respect them and use them wisely. It is to everyone's advantage to know the facts and respect the land. Educate your fellow bikers. It is our responsibility to stop our friends from careless and destructive use of the trails.

Various organizations are popping up world-wide to help educate and support mountain biking by promoting responsible riding and trail preservation. Probably the largest is the International Mountain Biking Association (IMBA). Formed in 1988, IMBA has been a successful advocate for the sport of mountain biking.

On a local level, Hawai'i has its own success story. Hawai'i Bicycling League (HBL), established in the 1960s, has been our advocate for recreational and functional bicycling. HBL's administration now plays an important role as an advocate for mountain biking as well. In 1989, HBL, in cooperation with the State of Hawai'i Department of Education formed a program called "BikeEd." BikeEd has become part of the elementary school curriculum for 4th graders. The students are taught general biking techniques, traffic laws and safety. Equipped with helmets and bikes, they have five 45 minute sessions with two certified instructors.

Educational programs for children like this one are important for the future of mountain biking. Teaching today's cyclists common sense and the importance of responsible riding will keep our trails open and safe for future generations to enjoy.

Proper riding techniques

Damage to trails caused by erosion and accelerated by mountain bikers is usually confined to certain fragile sections, such as steep hills and various puddling areas. In these sections of trail, proper riding techniques will help minimize impact.

Proper techniques require the control of your own bike. Maintaining traction is the foremost requirement. Nobby tires are designed to hold firm to the trail and are a must for mountain bikes. As long as your tires don't lose traction and the terrain is dry, erosion is at a bare minimum.

Knowing the stopping distance of your bike is especially important when going down a steep hill. Skidding or sliding will cause the tire to rip at the surface soil and increase erosion. On steep sections of trail, a skidding bicycle tire wears down the surface, eventually creating a small rut. The rut will become enlarged when it rains and water funnels down it. If the rut is not filled, the trail will become increasingly damaged by rain and other trail users. To avoid skidding, use both the front and rear brakes together and lean back to keep your weight over the rear wheel. If the hill is too steep, dismount and walk your bike down it. When accelerating or climbing a hill, again keep your weight over the rear wheel and stay in a higher gear to prevent loss of traction. Up-shifting into a higher gear makes it a little harder to pedal, but will help keep your rear wheel from spinning out during acceleration.

Puddles caused by poor drainage will remain long after the rain. Riding or stomping through these areas makes things worse. When you encounter a mud puddle, dismount and carefully hike your bike around the puddled area to prevent further damage, but try not to trample the vegetation.

A rider demonstrates proper uphill technique.

Proper riding techniques also include controlling your speed. Besides increasing your stopping distance and risk, speed can loosen roots and rocks that help to hold the soil in place. Speed may threaten your safety and the safety of other trail users. When visibility is poor, such as at turns and in dark areas of a trail, slow down and travel at a low speed so you can stop quickly, if necessary.

If we all ride safely, preserve trails and help to reduce user conflicts, mountain bikers will be welcomed and closed trails may be reopened for everyone to enjoy. With this in mind, ride with a smile and help educate others with your positive attitude and knowledge.

A rider dismounts to avoid mud.

Get involved in trail maintenance

Before a trail is made, raw forest, dense vegetation and steep grades are the norm. Before the first tree is cut, many days of research are spent to determine the environmental impact of the proposed trail. State conservationists conduct environmental and archeological assessments, while botanists inspect the area for rare and endangered species. Once the trail is approved, a team of volunteers and a handful of paid person-

Mountain bikers and hikers work together to maintain a trail.

nel begin cutting the trail that sometimes takes years to complete. Volunteer trail crews finish their day's work with blisters, sunburn and exhaustion, but accompanied by a feeling of great accomplishment. The men and women who volunteer their time to blaze the trails that we bike on are dedicated people who enjoy what they are doing. Their efforts allow others, such as you and I, to enjoy a safe and accessible trail.

According to Na Ala Hele, the Maunawili Trail, on Oʻahu's windward side, cost the state $50,000 to build. Over one thousand Sierra Club volunteers spent three years to blaze seven miles of new trail. Depending on the difficulty of the terrain, approximately 20 volunteers moved at pace of about 500 feet per day. Yet, with all of this time and money, natural erosion began to take place from day one.

All trails suffer from natural erosion caused by the elements such as rain, wind and water run off. Hikers, bikers and in some cases equestrians, speed up this erosion process. Eroded problem areas of trails where water run-off is great and steep grades exist need constant maintenance. Overhead canopy's of lush growth block out the drying effects of the sun and the trail retains the moisture.

Some of these areas have been under reconstruction with the addition of waterbars and/or boardwalks. Water bars are made from large tree branches, trunks or synthetic material and are placed diagonally across the trail, partially sunk into the ground. They direct water off the trail and slow bikers down. Some trails that have exceptionally steep terrain are modified with log steps that resemble waterbars. Boardwalks have been constructed on certain areas of trails with poor drainage. Here the biker doesn't even touch the ground below. This has proven to be the most effective device to prevent further damage.

Maintenance is important in the quest for lasting, functional and safe trails. The State and some private organizations work together to maintain trails. This gives people like us a chance to volunteer and be a part of the solution and not the problem. As a trail user, an opportunity to help maintain trails is one of the best ways to give back something to the community.

IMBA has compiled a collection of literary resources for trail development and construction which are being used in Hawai'i to restore existing trails. Their illustrated book contains technical information on trail design for heavily used trails.

Where ever you live, you can make a difference by getting involved in trail maintenance. Contact your local bike clubs or forestry department for information on how you can help.

4 Mountain Biking Safety

Hazards

Blended in with the beauty of Hawai'i's outdoors lies the unexpected. When you are mountain biking, you need to be aware of your surroundings and watch out for hikers and dangerous areas of the trail. Anytime you venture off the smooth asphalt onto a mountain trail, you will encounter a different set of hazards. Typically, roots, rocks and cliffs are the most common dangers. Watch the trail surface and keep an eye out for changes in terrain and protruding objects. Tree stumps and boulders are sometimes hidden among the shrubs and grass. If you were to accidentally catch one of these with your tire or pedal, you could be thrown from your bike. You know the saying, "it's not the fall that hurts you, it's that sudden stop." You should always be wearing safety gear, which is covered in the Safety Accessories section.

The weather can change rapidly, sending showers of rain that will turn your trail surface into a slippery hazard. If you get caught in the rain, expect roots and rocks to become slick as ice. During heavy rains, stream levels can rise up over certain sections of trails. Flash floods can occur without warning and can be life-threatening. Use extreme caution near streams and waterfalls.

The water from the streams and puddles may contain leptospirosis and other bacteria. Drinking stream water is not recommended unless it is treated, boiled or filtered with an adequate filtering device. Swimming or riding with open wounds can lead to infection and/or illness caused from leptospirosis. Contact the State Division of Forestry and Wildlife for further information.

Recreational vehicles are permitted on some roads and can be a hazard to bikers. Motorcycles, All Terrain Vehicles (ATV's) and 4WD trucks move fast. Never assume that they see you. Stay alert. Look and listen for approaching motorized vehicles and move out of their way.

Deep in our valleys, hunters roam the forests with crossbows and guns, searching for pigs and game birds. Bikers are advised to stay on the main trail to avoid entering a hunting zone.

Rock Climbing

The volcanic rock in Hawai'i's mountains is a hazard for those who enjoy rock climbing. Our volcanic rock is brittle and crumbles easily. For your own safety, do not attempt to leave the safety of the trail to climb cliffs.

Getting lost

It does happen now and then to folks who leave the trail and lose their sense of direction. The following tips should help you avoid becoming a lost mountain biker:
- Darkness sets in fast after sunset, so don't begin your mountain adventures late in the day.
- Stay on the main trail.
- Use a map and/or compass.
- Pack a mini-survival kit and carry a cellular phone and flashlight for emergencies.
- Never bike or hike alone.

Mountain biking safety tips

Safety should always be a major consideration in every sport, so consider the following before mountain biking. Know your bike and familiarize yourself with its handling characteristics. Practice stopping, turning and shifting in both wet and dry conditions. When down shifting gears on an uphill, be sure not to apply too much pressure on the pedals during your shift. This can snap your chain or chip teeth on your chainring and/or cogs. An early down shift just before a grade steepens or shifting while the bike still has momentum will remedy this. Stay seated while shifting to prevent an accident in case your chain slips and you miss the next gear. If this happens, you will experience a hyper-speed rotation of the the crank arm which could lead to a fall.

A rider negotiates steep and uneven terrain.

Adjusting your seat to the proper height for different terrain also aides in comfort and maneuverability. Your foot should rest flat on the pedal at the down stroke with only a slight bend of the knee. If you are riding a steep downhill or practicing your trials techniques, try dropping your seat lower and you'll find that your mobility of the bike increases.

When mountain biking on single tracks, stay on the trail.

Always ride with a friend and tell others where you are going and what time you're expected back. Don't make last minute changes to your plans without telling someone. In the unlikely event that you would need rescue assistance, rescue teams would find you much faster if they knew exactly where to look. Carry a cellular phone in case you need to communicate due to an emergency. This safety feature has saved many and likely will save many more. If you have an emergency, call 911 and ask for the Honolulu Fire Department. They will activate their ground and air rescue personnel to assist you.

Don't be a brave, "NO FEAR" type of off-road warrior unless you are willing to suffer the consequences. If an area of a trail looks too critical for your skill level, dismount and walk your bike. There are many steep cliffs on our trails, and you should always be cautious, especially if you are an amateur. Many of our trails are narrow single tracks, so ride with caution and don't take any unnecessary risks. Riding should be fun! Don't push yourself or your buddy to do anything that threatens your personal safety. Ride at speeds that match the terrain and your skill level so that you can easily slow and stop if needed.

When you encounter other trail users such as, hikers, equestrians or recreational vehicle drivers, be prepared to stop or ask if you may pass. When approaching equestrians, it is especially important that you do not spook the horses. They are much bigger than you and can be easily be startled. If you see equestrians ahead, stop to the side of the trail and let them pass. If you are traveling in the same direction, maintain the same speed as the horses, but keep your distance and ask the rider if it is alright to pass. If so, all bikers should pass on the same side of the horse to avoid confusing the animal.

Safety accessories

Wearing safety gear while mountain biking is a must. Your bike has been built to withstand the stress of off-roading. Suspension can be added to diminish shock caused by bumps and uneven terrain. Padded saddles help to add comfort to your 'okole (butt) while riding and nobby tires improve traction on dirt and mud.

Given all the improvements we make to our bikes, it makes sense that we should improve our personal protection as well. Safety gear helps to prevent injury in case of accident. Experienced mountain bikers know that, "it's not if you fall, it's when you fall". Probably the highest priority is to protect your head. Find yourself a helmet that is comfortable and fits properly. Check for the ANSI or SNELL labels that show the helmet has passed regulated safety specifications. Have your local bike shop help select one that is right for you.

Goggles or sunglasses are helpful to protect your eyes. Flying insects, rocks, dirt, branches and even bright sunlight are hazards that eye protection helps to deal with. For the safety conscious rider, shin guards, elbow pads, knee pads and full face shields are additional equipment that further protection.

Selecting appropriate biking shoes is also important. Along

Always wear protective safety gear.

with comfort and proper fit, your shoes must have nobby soles for traction. Some riders prefer hiking shoes while others choose specially designed biking shoes with a binding system. Never ride with slippers or sandals.

Before you ride

Use the following check list to ensure a successful ride. This may seem like a lot of preparation, but it should be standard practice.

- Before you ride, a good meal is as vital as putting fuel in your car. Your body will need the energy to get you over the hill and back again.
- Stretching is a great warm-up and helps to prevent muscle injury.
- Bring your helmet, shoes, gloves, shades, sunscreen, full water bottle (or camel back), and foul weather gear (as needed).
- You should always carry a small tool bag which includes pump, tire patch kit, chain breaker, allen wrench set with flathead and phillips screwdrivers attached, 10mm wrench and tire pries.
- Additional equipment may include an extra tire tube, a light for night riders, snacks for the long rides, a first aid kit (bee sting kit or medications as needed) and a cellular phone for emergencies.
- Check your tire pressure (suggested p.s.i. is labeled on tire), shock pressure and adjustable settings and tighten any loose hardware.

Now, you are ready for the trail. Have fun!

5 Bicycle Maintenance

Maintaining your mountain bike

Your mountain bike should be well maintained and lubricated at all times. Components that are well kept will give you much more accurate responses and last longer. Schedule regular maintenance for your bike. Owning your own tools and knowing how to use them should help to minimize the overhaul and repair costs.

Check all bolts and connections before and after each ride and tighten any loose hardware as needed. Inspect and repack the bearings in your headset, bottom bracket and hubs at least once a year. Do this more often if you are riding regularly in wet and muddy conditions.

Bearing grease such as Bullshot® and Finish Line® are formulated specifically for bicycle use. Some riders use a more water resilient grease designed for boat trailers but, it is more viscous and tends to create unneeded drag.

The headset takes a lot of abuse and can sometimes become loose. To check it, lock the front brake by pulling the lever tight. Roll the bike forward and backward to feel for play in the headset. If you feel play, tighten the headset immediately.

Wheel hubs can be checked by holding the bike firmly and moving the rim laterally. Use the same check for the bottom bracket. Grab the crank arm and move it laterally to check for play.

Brake and shifting cables should be greased within the cable housing when possible. Worn, rusty or frayed cables are dangerous and can snap at critical moments. Don't wait. If these inexpensive items are worn, replace them.

Chains take a lot of stress and should be inspected often for rust and deformities. Chains can be checked with a special tool that is made to measure the amount of stretch in the chain. This will help to determine replacement needs. Lubricate the chain as often as possible and especially after wet and muddy rides. Use a good Teflon lubricant like Tri-Flow® for your chain and derailleurs.

Correct derailleur adjustment provides smooth and accurate shifting. If your derailleur doesn't line up with cogs or sprockets, an obvious grinding or clicking noise will remind you that an adjustment is needed.

Inspect your brake pads to be sure that they are set properly. Otherwise, you will hear the "mountain bike mating call". Improper adjustment can also lead to brake failure or sudden tire wall blow out.

If you have a suspension package on your bike, check

under the boots for any leaky cylinders and clean out dust and debris. Inspect the crown and mount for stress cracks and loose bolts. The suspension absorbs shock and impact and deserves routine inspection. Suspension products should only be serviced by an authorized dealer.

Even with the high-tech engineering of today's frames, stress cracks and broken frames are still a part of life. Riding styles which include jumping, drop-offs, hard crashes and collisions can lead to frame damage. Stressed areas can be found during routine cleaning.

Check your tires for worn side walls, ballooning and imbedded objects. A high speed blow out is something to be reckoned with.

Lift the bike and free spin the wheels to check for rim deformities. Out of round or cracked rims should be replaced and out of "true" rims should be repaired. Bent, loose or broken spokes can weaken a rims integrity. Replace any bad spokes.

If you do not have the time or the patience to be a grease monkey, take your bike to the professionals for service. With a routine maintenance program, you'll enjoy more time on the trail than off it.

Cleaning your bike

Keeping your mountain bike clean and well lubricated will enhance the life of your paint, components and accessories. Simple Green®, diluted with water, makes an excellent cleaning solution. Use a wet sponge or cloth to apply soap to the bike, then rinse thoroughly with water. Try to avoid mixing concentrated soap with lubricants and bearings.

On shoreline trails, you can expect to be subjected to a high level of salt spray, so you should wash your bike the same day you rode it. Sand is gritty and washes off quite easily. If you leave the sand on your bike, it will add wear on brakes, rims, chain and sprockets, so clean as often as possible.

The primary soil compound at Ka'ena Point and Kahuku is like clay. On dry days it is no problem and a lot of fun to ride on. However, if it rains, your ride will soon be over. This stuff sticks to your tires, spokes, chain, brakes and shoes. You will end up walking your bike, your footwear will resemble platform shoes and your tires, well, good luck... Most of the time, 15 to 25 feet is the maximum distance your tires will roll before you have to scrape  the mud off. When it gets bad, hopefully you won't be too far from a paved road or civilization.

Cleaning your bike after riding it in wet clay is a major chore. It is best to wait a day and let the mud dry. Then break off the dried chunks and add them to your garden. Your chain, derailleurs and cables should always be lubricated after every cleaning to ensure that they operate smoothly.

6 Hawai'i's Competition Scene

Then and now

When mountain biking first became popular in Hawai'i during the early 1980's, competitive spirit ran through the hearts of only a few off-road warriors. Mountain bike racing  was usually just between a few friends. With increased interest in this exciting sport, it was not long before the first official competitions were held.

In 1984, the first off-road event on O'ahu was put on by Jill Cheever (now Wheatman) and The Bike Way. Deep in the cane fields of Helemano, a small event was held on military property with their permission. The race attracted 70 riders, many of them street cyclists or roadies.

In 1986, Curt Evans of Hale'iwa began holding regularly scheduled events. Curt ran three events per year under the "Down/Up" name which he still uses. The biggest thing to happen in mountain biking at that time was getting on national television during the Supercross motorcycle race that was held at Aloha Stadium in 1986. During intermission, a mountain bike race was held on the motorcycle track, giving mountain biking in Hawai'i national recognition.

During the fall of 1987, the original "Mauka Bike Club" was formed and began their racing events. A funny thing happened however, during the "Kahuku Enduro" in November 1987. Poor trail markings left riders scrambling to find the course. One poor competitor was found scared up a tree by a feral pig. The race was held over until the following weekend.

In 1989, The Bike Way Challenge at Kahuku was rained out early race morning. The competitors showed up, but were discouraged to find out that Kahuku mud sticks like glue. The access road to the race track was impassible by 2WD and bicycles. The few racers and organizers who camped overnight found themselves alone with a lot of donated food. The food soon became the ammo of a huge food fight. This race was also held over to the following weekend.

Hans Rey, a nationally known "trials" expert, came to Hawai'i in 1989 to oversee a trials clinic and watch over the "No-Dab" trials event at Kahuku. Trials events feature a slow moving, technical style of riding which requires perfect balance, coordination and complete control of the bicycle. The object is to clear a section of obstacles consisting of boulders, roots, rocks, lumber, trees and for Hans, automobiles. Penalty points are given to riders each time they "dab". A dab is defined as any part of your body that touches a solid object or ground to regain balance. The fewest points determines the winner. To "clean" a section means that the rider maneuvered through a section without dabbing.

Over the years, other local race

Competitor Ken Mackie takes a practice lap.

organizers such as Scott Chaney of Semi-Boneless Racing, Bill Barnfield of Raging Isle, John Mathias of HBL and Tracy Paiwa of Mauka Bike Club have put on a number of events which generated increased enthusiasm for mountain biking. Race directors expanded race locations to include Kahuku, Ka'ena Point and Bellows Air Force Base. Combining events such as uphills, downhills, trials, cross countries, and time trials, interest spread to the neighbor islands and the list of competitors grew. Each event began drawing 50 to 100 riders and proved that the sport was here to stay. The top local riders in the late 1980's included Ray Brust, Chris Clark, Brian Thomas, Darrell Aki, Robert Terines, Steve Delacruz, and Pamela Nevitt.

Hawaiian Mountain Tour Pro/Am 1995. Twain Newhart photo.

In 1991, when the National Off-Road Bicycling Association (NORBA) sponsored its first event in Hawai'i, organized mountain biking reached a new level in securing race locations. NORBA is a non-profit organization that promotes mountain bike racing nationwide. NORBA-sanctioned events are insured and adhere to strict guidelines. NORBA's presence helped to legitimize local races which in turn has helped to access private property for other events.

Hawai'i's NORBA representative, John Farrrar, has been organizing and promoting mountain bike competitions here with continued success. With approximately 18 NORBA events held statewide during 1995, the future of mountain bike racing in Hawai'i looks bright. John notes that Hawai'i has a very strong competitive group. Riders such as O'ahu's Joey Riviera, Chris Clark, Ray Brust and Bradley Lastimosa, Michelle Foster and Karen Shimmin, Kaua'i's Joe McNerny, Maui's J.R. Roberts, and the Big Island's Chris Seymour, Mike French, and Garuda McCarthy are some of the names to remember in the races to come.

Since races are only held where harm to the environment is not an issue, the "go slowly, don't skid your rear wheel and be careful of hikers" theory doesn't apply. On race day, it's time to kick some butt! The Hawaiian Mountain Tour Pro/Am was a good example of such an event. Sponsored by Outrigger Hotels of Hawai'i and organized by Event Marketing, this was by far Hawai'i's biggest mountain biking event. The four day event included a prologue time trial, a point-to-point, a circuit race, a downhill and a criterium. Pro rider, Thomas Frischknecht won first place overall while Juli Furtado placed first in the women's Pro event. The spectacular setting for this race was world famous Ka'a'awa Valley at Kualoa Ranch and the North Shore's Waimea Valley. These two private properties offered a wide variety of tropical terrain and scenery. Both valleys have a utopia of single tracks with warm stream crossings and fast and wild 4WD roads. All of this and an island paradise background also created a photographic opportunity which pleased riders, promoters and sponsors so much that Hawai'i was awarded the World Cup Finals for 1996.

For further information on local competitions, refer to Bike Clubs in the back of this book for contact numbers.

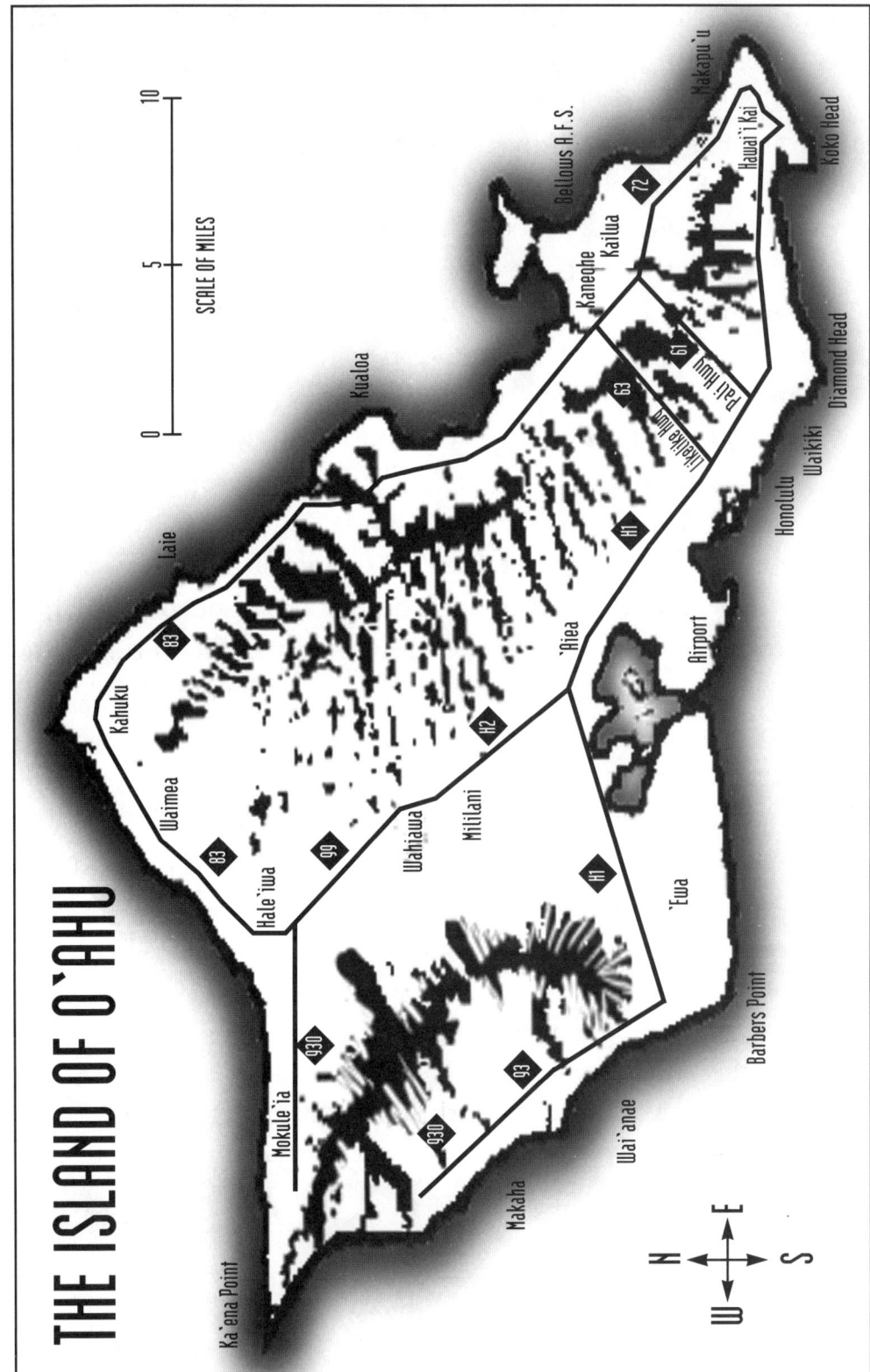

LEGEND FOR MAPS

ICONS:

 TREES & FOREST — CLIFF HAZARD
 ROOTS AND ROCKS — DROP OFF
 OFF-CAMBER — JUMPS
 GUAVA GROVE — DISMOUNT
 VIEW POINT — FOOT PATH ONLY
 PARKING — MOUNTAIN BIKE
 UPHILL — BAMBOO FOREST
 DOWNHILL — LOOSE GRAVEL
 ELEVATIONS — SIGNS
 DISTANCE IN MILES — ULUHE FERN

DIFFICULTY RATINGS:

♦♦♦ ADVANCED
♦♦ INTERMEDIATE
♦ BEGINNER

TRAIL & ROAD MARKINGS:

――――― SINGLE TRACK
·············· FOOT PATH ONLY
▬▬▬▬▬ PAVED ROAD
•••••••••••• 4WD ROAD

LOCATION MAP:

THE ARROW POINTS TO THE LOCATION OF TRAIL

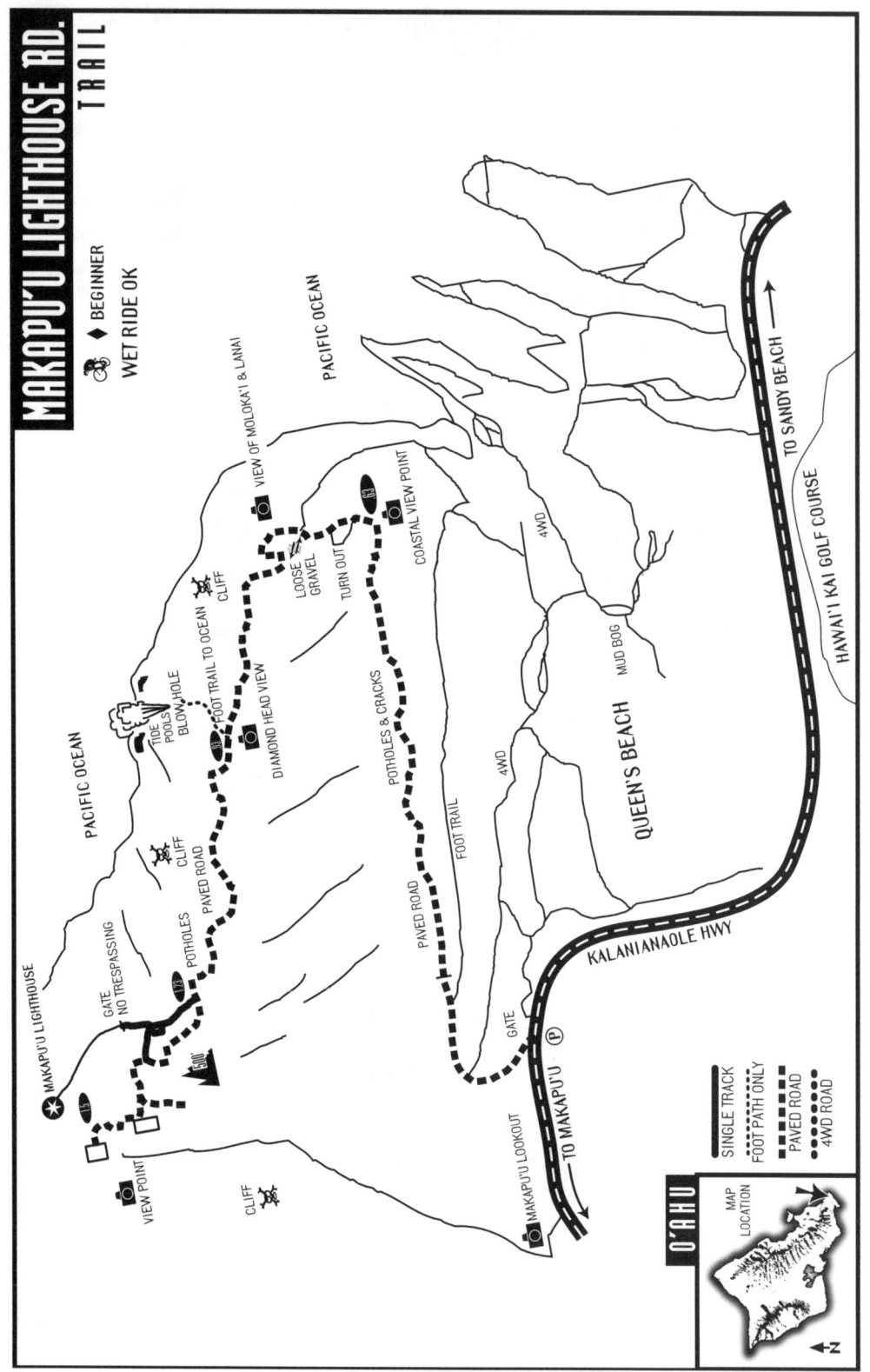

Makapuʻu Lighthouse Road

How to get there: Located at the easternmost tip of Oʻahu's Koʻolau Range. Follow Kalanianaʻole Hwy 72 east-bound approximately two miles past Sandy Beach Park. Paved access begins between Hawaiʻi Kai Golf Course and Makapuʻu Lookout. Park off the highway and do not leave valuables in car. Carry your bike around the locked gate and proceed up the paved road.

Makapuʻu Lighthouse Road: 3.0 miles round trip
Rating: Beginner
Special: Permit not needed.
Note: Paved road only. Wet ride ok.
Hazards: Unmaintained paved road. Deep cracks, potholes, loose gravel and cliffs.
Amenities: None
History: Now automated, lighthouse used to be manned.
Elevation range: 500 feet

This is a scenic uphill ride to the Makapuʻu Lighthouse viewpoint. You will most likely encounter other bikers and hikers, so be prepared to slow or stop, especially on the downhill run. Beautiful scenic views are found on the entire length of the road. The dry coastal environment is home for cactus, kiawe and haole koa trees. The first viewpoint is just beyond the second gate at about the .63 mile mark. (see map) Below to your right is the Queen's Beach area. From this elevated view, many dirt roads and trails can be seen. Down the coast about two miles is Sandy Beach Park, one of the best sites for bodysurfing, bodyboarding and skimboarding.

At the .73 mile mark, you will be able to look out over the Ka'iwi or Moloka'i Channel. The islands of Moloka'i and Lana'i are usually visible. On a clear day, Maui's Haleakala "house of the sun" can be seen hiding behind the eastern tip of Moloka'i. Between the months of November and May, you might see some passing humpback whales breaching in the blue Pacific. On occasion, seabirds like albatross', frigates and boobies fly by in search of the day's fresh catch.

Proceed further up past two hairpin turns and you will come to a white concrete block on the right (approx. .93 mile mark). On your left is a great view of two dormant volcanos. The closer one is Koko Crater. Off in the distance is Le'ahi or Diamond Head which sits next to Waikiki. On the right side of the road, you'll see a small painted arrow which points down the cliff. This marks a trail head, but is for hikers only. Do not attempt the trail on a bike. It ascends a steep cliff comprised of loose rocks and gravel to a cluster of blow holes and small tide pools at sea level. This area is very hazardous during big surf, so stay clear during high surf episodes.

Proceeding further, the paved road splits off to the right (approx. 1.23 mile mark). This is a closed entrance to the lighthouse. Only Coast Guard personnel are allowed beyond the locked gate.

The top of the road is the end of this short ride. Two platforms with hand rails have been constructed for safe viewing of the jagged sea cliffs below. The higher platform has the best view of the historic Makapu'u Lighthouse below to the right. Two islands are visible below. The smaller is Kaohikaipu or Black Rock and the larger is Manana Island or Rabbit Island. Both of them are state bird refuges. Makapu'u Beach and Sea Life Park are below to the left. Standing here, you can visualize the shoreline from

Waimanalo to Ka'a'awa and the Mokulua Islands off of Kailua. The prominent three pointed peak in the distance is Olomana which is the finish point of the Maunawili Trail.

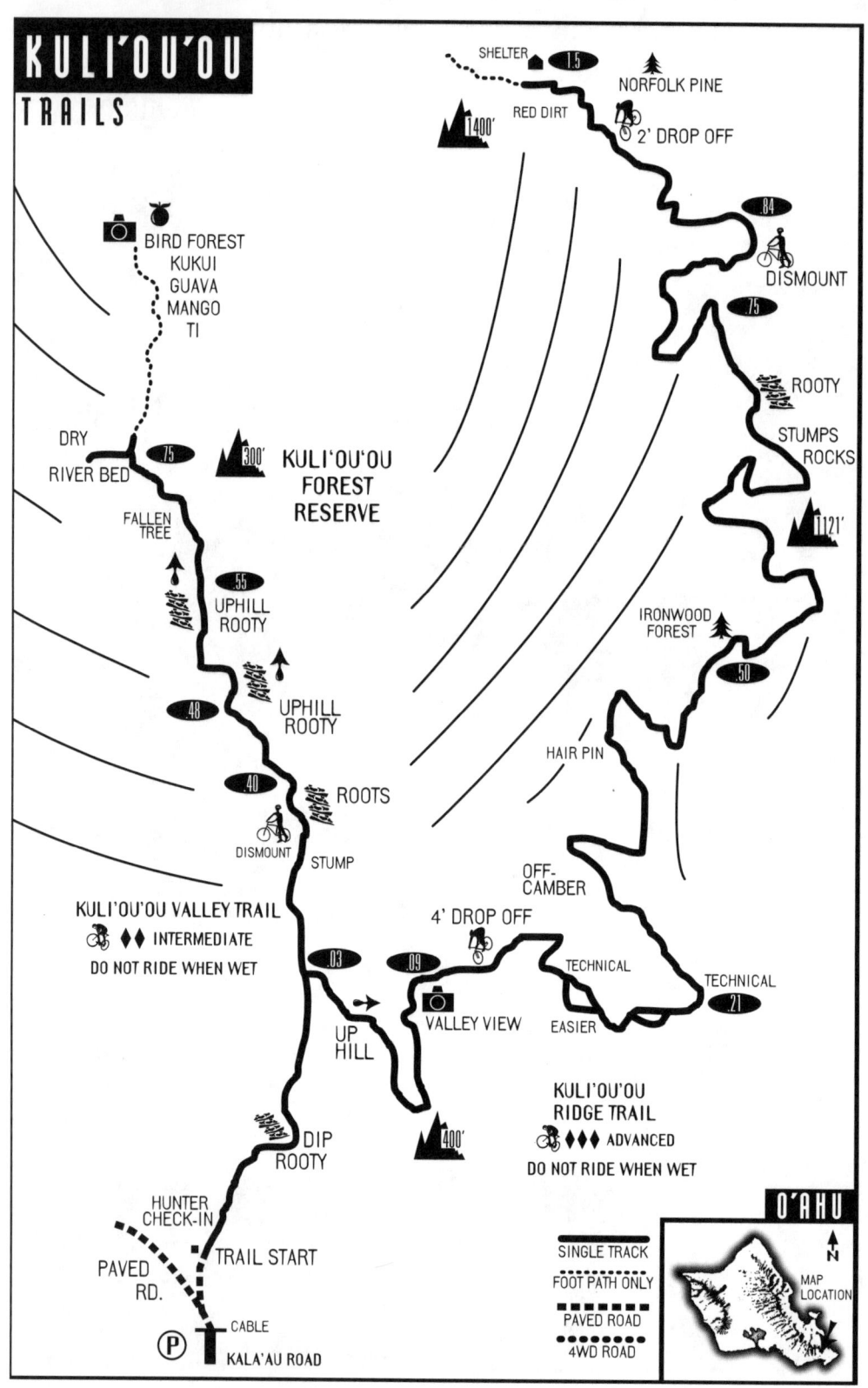

Kuliʻouʻou Trails

How to get there: Located on southeastern Oʻahu, Kuliʻouʻou lies between Hawaiʻi Kai and Niu Valley. Traveling on Kalanianaʻole Hwy 72, turn mauka on Kuliʻouʻou Road and proceed about a mile into the valley. Turn right on Kalaʻau Place and park at the end of the road. Pass the cable and go right at the fork. Continue past the hiker check-in station to access both trails.

Kuliʻouʻou Valley Trail: 1.25 miles round trip
Rating: Intermediate (with dismounts)
Special: No permit needed. Stay on main trail.
Note: Single track. DO NOT ride when wet or raining.
Hazards: Cliffs, loose terrain, flooding and hunters in valley.
Amenities: None
Elevation range: 300 feet

This is a short trail which follows the valley floor along the right side of the stream bed. Slightly bumpy and off camber terrain with an abundance of roots and rocks. Use caution if you get caught in the rain as this trail is slippery when wet. When you reach the .75 mile mark, a footpath proceeds through very rocky terrain. The valley becomes quite lush with a variety of ferns, kukui, mango and guava trees. For bird watchers, the valley is full of song by our fine feathered friends.

Kuliʻouʻou Ridge Trail: 3.0 miles round-trip
Rating: Advanced (with dismounts)
Special: No permit needed. Stay on main trail.
Note: Single track. DO NOT ride when wet or raining.
Hazards: Cliffs, roots, rocks, loose terrain and hunters in valley.
Amenities: Picnic table with shelter at top of single track.

History: Trail was cut in 1990.

Elevation range: 1,400 feet

A challenging uphill ride that zigzags up the right side of the valley. Cliffs exist along most of the trail, so use caution. Some difficult areas with roots and rocks are found in various spots along this winding trail. The hairpin turns and drop-off sections can be trying for anyone, even with years of experience. There are a few sections which will require dismounting, but most of the trail is ridable and fun.

The trail ends up at a shelter with two picnic tables. There is a cleared section of red dirt that's good for messing around and practicing your trials techniques.

The trail continues past the shelter for a short distance before turning into an arduous foot trail. The trail ascends the final peak to the summit where the view of Waimanalo is well worth the hike. No bikes allowed on summit trail. The downhill is a blast, but as always, watch for hikers.

Wiliwilinui Ridge Trail

How to get there: Located above Wai'alae Iki on O'ahu's south shore. Turn mauka off Kalaniana'ole Hwy 72 and head up Laukahi Street. Approximately 1.6 miles up, you will come to a guard shack where you will get your day pass. Continue up Laukahi to the end and turn left on Okoa Street. Proceed to the end of the paved road and park. Be sure to observe signs and parking restrictions. Keep your day pass on the driver's side of your dashboard. The cable across the road marks the beginning of the Wiliwilinui Ridge Trail.

Wiliwilinui Ridge Trail: 3.2 miles round trip
Rating: Intermediate (with dismounts)
Special: No permit needed. A day pass from the guard shack on Laukahi Street is necessary.
Note: 4WD dirt road. Wet ride ok. No bikes on summit trail.
Hazards: Cliffs, possible 4WD's, loose terrain, slippery when wet.
Amenities: Parking
Elevation range: 1,800 feet

   The Ko'olau Range offers many valleys and ridges to explore. This special bike trek is a must for mountain biking enthusiasts. The first 1.6 miles of this trail is a 4WD road and is plenty wide for mountain bikes to ride side by side. A variety of uphills and downhills along with some rutted out areas make for an exciting ride. Mud puddles are common along this road and may be deeper than they appear. Seasonal strawberry guavas are found along the road side to nibble on. As you near the end of the road, watch for some fantastic valley views.

   At the end of the road, a foot trail marks the final climb to the summit. No bikes are allowed on the summit trail. If

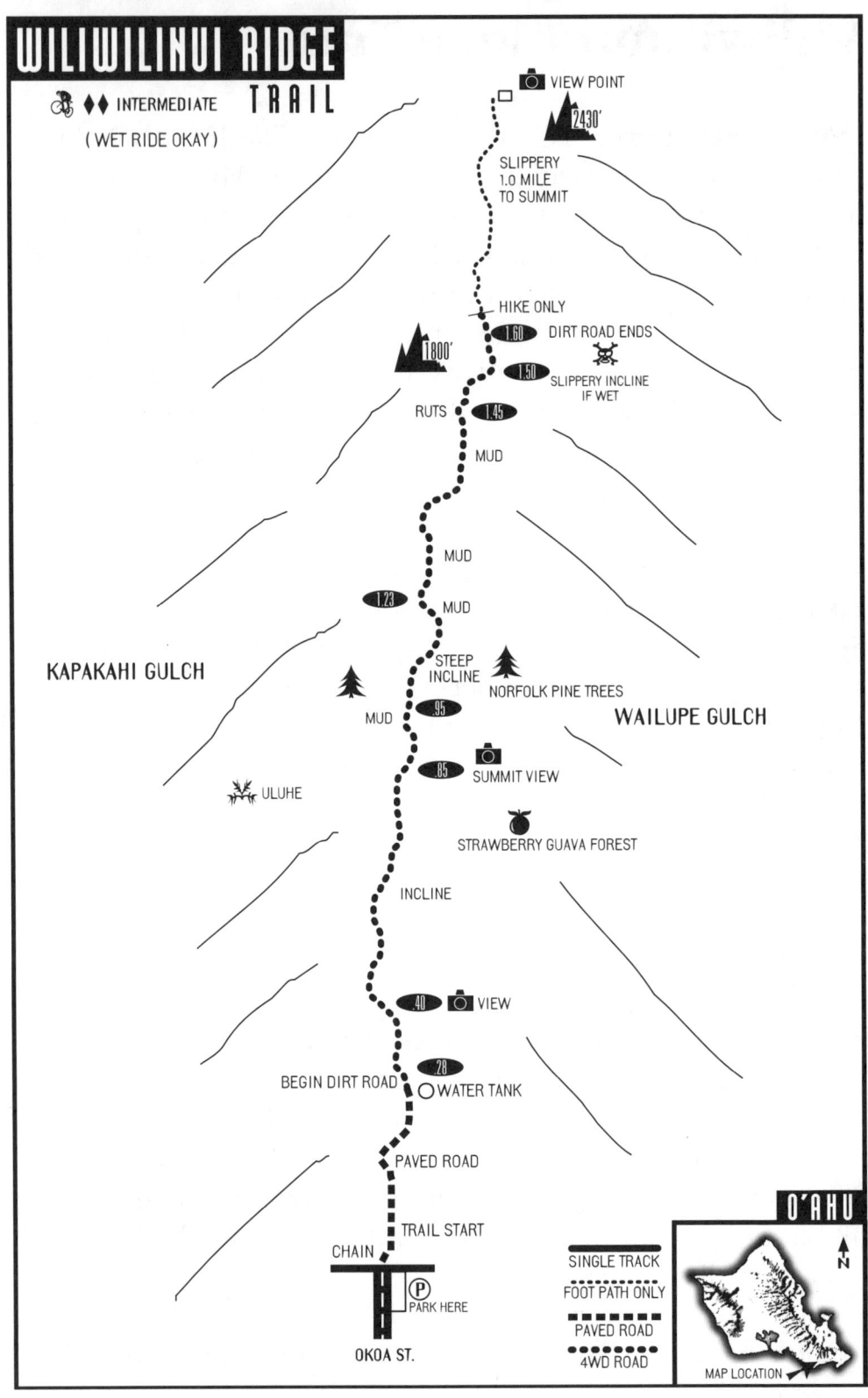

you decide to lock your bike and continue on foot, a one hour uphill climb will bring you to the Wiliwilinui communications repeater on the ridge top. On a clear day, you will have an excellent view of Waimanalo and Olomana on the windward side. Looking back at the leeward side, you will catch a spectacular view from Hawai'i Kai to Makakilo. Always remember to stay on the main trail and don't attempt to get too close to cliff areas. The ground is moist and slippery and is dangerous near steep sections.

Your return trip will go by much quicker. Be careful on the hike down and don't take chances. Once you've reached your bike, a quick brake check would be appropriate before the downhill. Some short pedaling will be necessary but, fear not, the downhill sections are exhilarating and fast. Use caution near the rutted out areas and puddles. Watch for hikers around blind curves.

The view of 'Aina Haina from Wiliwilinui Ridge Trail.

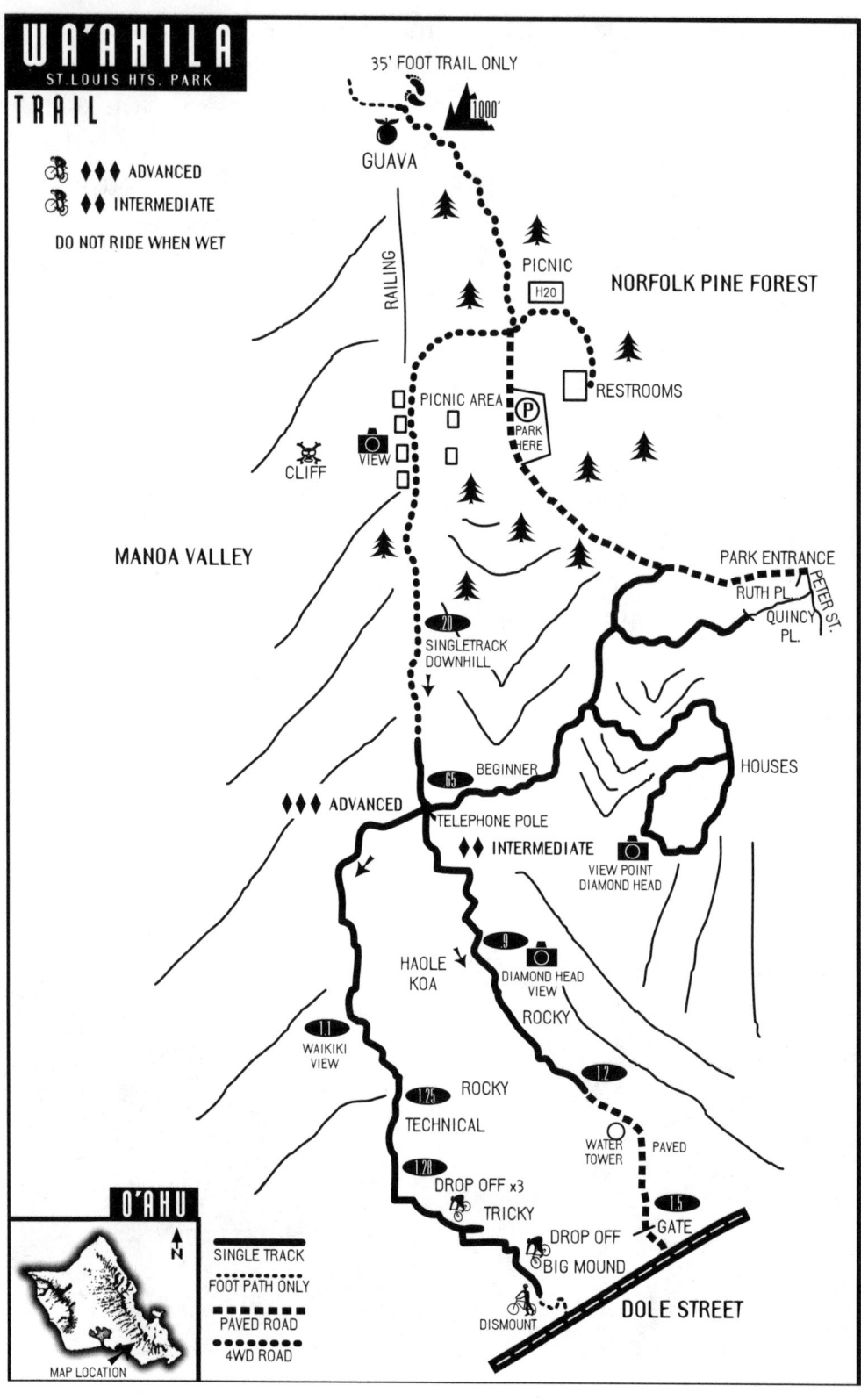

Wa'ahila Trail

How to get there: Located above Kaimuki on O'ahu's south shore. From Wai'alae Avenue, turn mauka onto St. Louis Heights Drive. Follow road to the top and turn right onto Peter Street and left onto Ruth Place. Pass the gated entrance to Wa'ahila State Park. Gate is open from 7am to 7:30pm. If you're planning on staying after the park is closed, park your car outside the gate. The Wa'ahila Valley Trail will lead you to Dole Street at the bottom of St. Louis Heights. If you parked at the top parking lot, you will need to pedal back up via the trail or St. Louis Heights Drive.

Wa'ahila Valley Trails: 1.5 miles one way
Rating: Advanced (with dismounts)
 and Intermediate (with dismounts)
Special: No permit needed. Stay on main trail.
Note: Single track with some 4WD road. DO NOT ride when wet or raining.
Hazards: Cliffs, loose terrain, roots and rocks.
Amenities: Parking, shelter, tables, water and restrooms.
History: The Norfolk Pine forest was a reforestation project many years ago. The ridge top vegetation was destroyed by feral cattle in the early 1900's.
Elevation range: 1,000 feet

This is a short and sweet trail ride which winds down the ridge from the Norfolk Pine forest of Wa'ahila State Park. The first half mile is a dirt road that is loaded with roots and small drop-offs. The trail then becomes a single track, winding in and out of guava trees, eventually coming to a fork at a telephone pole.

The upper left trail will lead you back up to another fork

which will take you across a small valley of trees to a loop trail with a view.

By going straight at the telephone pole, you will ride down through a haole koa forest with some technical rocky sections and loose terrain. This is the easier way down to Dole Street. Potential development of this area may change the exit point.

If you were to hang a right at the telephone pole, you would end up following the ridge top down through dry haole koa forests. This is a technical and advanced route. At approximately the one mile mark, on your right is a beautiful view of Waikiki and the University of Hawai'i in Manoa Valley. Some thorny trees are found along this path, so use care when passing them. A quarter mile further and you'll come upon some advanced technical riding over and around a section of black rocks. Some drop-offs range from 2 to 8 feet with hidden rocks in the tall grass, so use caution and a helmet. Dismount when appropriate. The exit will require you to carry your bike down and out a narrow path to Dole Street.

Wa'ahila Ridge Trail: .35 miles one way
Rating: Intermediate
Special: No permit needed.
Note: 4WD road. Foot trail only beyond the .35 mile mark.
Hazards: Cliffs, steep and loose terrain.
Amenities: Parking, water, shelter, tables, restrooms.
Elevation range: 1,200 feet

The Wa'ahila Ridge Trail is only ridable up to the .35 mile mark. For bikers, it's a short uphill ride which passes through a forest of Norfolk Pine trees and strawberry guava trees. This short ride ends at a nice spot near the power lines. From here, the trail descends a steep ridge and is for hikers only.

Returning down to the park and connecting with the valley trails makes this uphill ride worth the effort.

Tantalus Trail System

Endangered Trails: The Tantalus Trail System is considered to be endangered. It is an extremely fragile trail system due to its moist environment and overuse. After careful consideration, I have elected to omit the trail maps of this area. The State Department of Land and Natural Resources, Division of Forestry and Wildlife has introduced a "rest period" for the Tantalus area. Select trails will be off-limits to mountain bikes during the rainy seasons.

The Tantalus Trail System consists of 14 different trails which includes the Arboretum Trail, Kanealole Trail, Maunalaha Trail, Nahuina Trail, Makiki Valley Trail, Ualakaa Trail, Moleka Trail, Manoa Cliff Trail, Pu'u 'Ohi'a Trail, Pauoa Flats Trail, Nu'uanu Trail, Judd Trail, Aihualama Trail and Manoa Falls Trail.

Restrictions for this area are subject to change. Inquire with DLNR--Na Ala Hele for up to date information. See Permit Information for contact number.

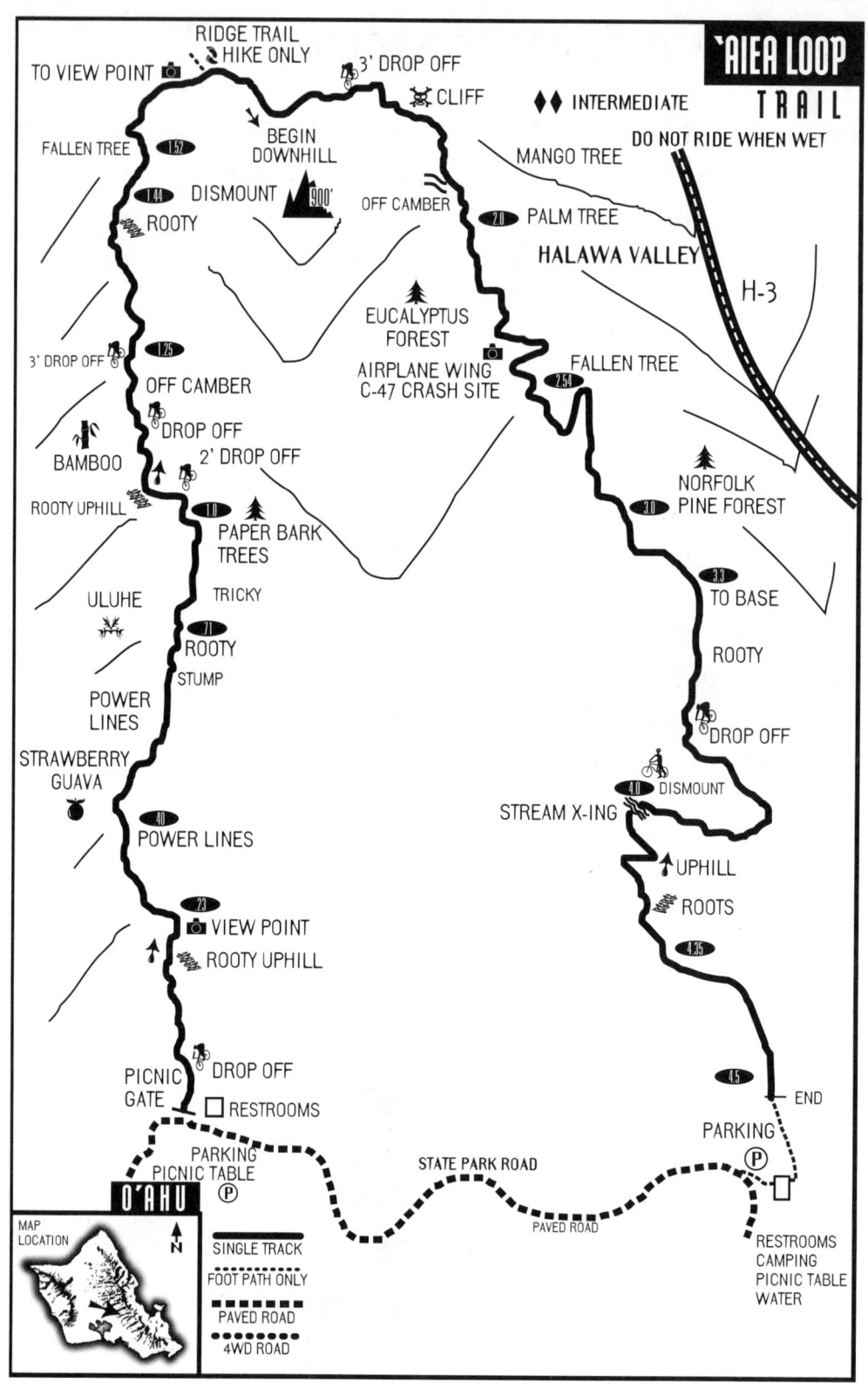

'Aiea Loop Trail

How to get there: Located above the town of 'Aiea. From Honolulu, take H-1 'ewa (west) bound and get off at exit 13A. Follow Moanalua Road. and turn right at 'Aiea Shopping Center. Follow 'Aiea Heights Drive past the gated entrance to Kea'iwa Heiau State Recreational Park. The upper trail head starts to the right, just left of the restrooms in the park at the crest of the hill.

'Aiea Loop Trail: 4.5 miles one way loop
Rating: Intermediate (with dismounts)
Special: No permit needed. Gate to park is open 7am-6:45pm/7am-7:45pm summer
Note: Single track. DO NOT ride if wet or raining.
Hazards: Cliffs, drop-offs, loose terrain, roots, rocks and hunters.
Amenities: Camping sites (permit only), parking, drinking water, restrooms, shelter and picnic tables.
History: Crash site of C-47 along trail. Kea'iwa Heiau is believed to be the ruins of an old medical healing site.
Elevation range: 900 feet

'Aiea Loop Trail is one of the most fun rides in central O'ahu. Although rated as an intermediate trail, there are many technical areas where you will need to dismount. Starting from the upper end (see map), you will drop into a small gully and climb the other side over a root bound technical uphill. The trail zigzags through some well shaded vegetation and ascends the ridge top.

Just before you begin the downhill at the 1.6 mile mark, the trail on your left begins the "hike only" ridge trail to the summit. A great rest stop to take in the view before descending the opposite ridge to the park.

This downhill has some dangerous cliff areas so be extremely careful. On the valley floor to your left lies the new H-3 freeway that connects the windward and leeward sides of the island.

On your right, at approx. 2.4 miles, you will encounter several pieces of an airplane. According to historians, these are the 1943 remnants of a military C-47 cargo plane which crashed shortly after take off. It was empty and all 3 crew members survived the frightening crash. It was enroute to Bellows AFS from Wheeler AFB.

Continuing down the switchback, you will finally reach the valley floor and stream crossing. Dismount and carry your bike across to ensure safety. A short uphill will return you to the lower trail head at the park. Follow the paved road up approx. 1/4 mile to your original starting position.

Manana Trail

How to get there: Located in Pacific Palisades, central Oʻahu. Heading north on H-1 freeway, take exit 10 Waimalu. Stay to the right and merge onto Moanalua Road. Proceed to the end and turn right at Waimano Home Road. Make a left at Komo Mai Road and follow to the end and park. Pass the locked gate and follow paved road to dirt trail head.

Manana Trail: 5.6 miles round trip
Rating: Intermediate (with dismounts)
Special: No permit needed. Stay on main trail.
Note: Single track. DO NOT ride if wet or raining.
Hazards: Cliffs, hunters, loose terrain, roots and rocks.
Amenities: Parking
Elevation range: 1,512 feet

An exceptional ride. The first .35 mile is a paved road. Just beyond the paved section, a beautiful single track continues up the ridge line. At approx. the .91 mile mark, the trail veers to the right, taking you to the beginning of a "hike only" trail that drops into Waimano Valley. Two beautiful pools with waterfalls lie at the bottom of the trail. Hike here another day when you aren't riding bikes.

Further up the ridge line at approx. 1.28 miles, the trail veers to the left and brings you out into the opening of another ridge. The first section is red dirt and is completely exposed. Ride further until you reach a steep cliff with a great view of Manana Valley. This is a perfect scenic overlook to break for lunch. On a clear day, the summits of the Koʻolau Range and the neighboring Waiʻanae Range show their multi-shades of green and steep cliffs. Both are beautiful, yet rugged.

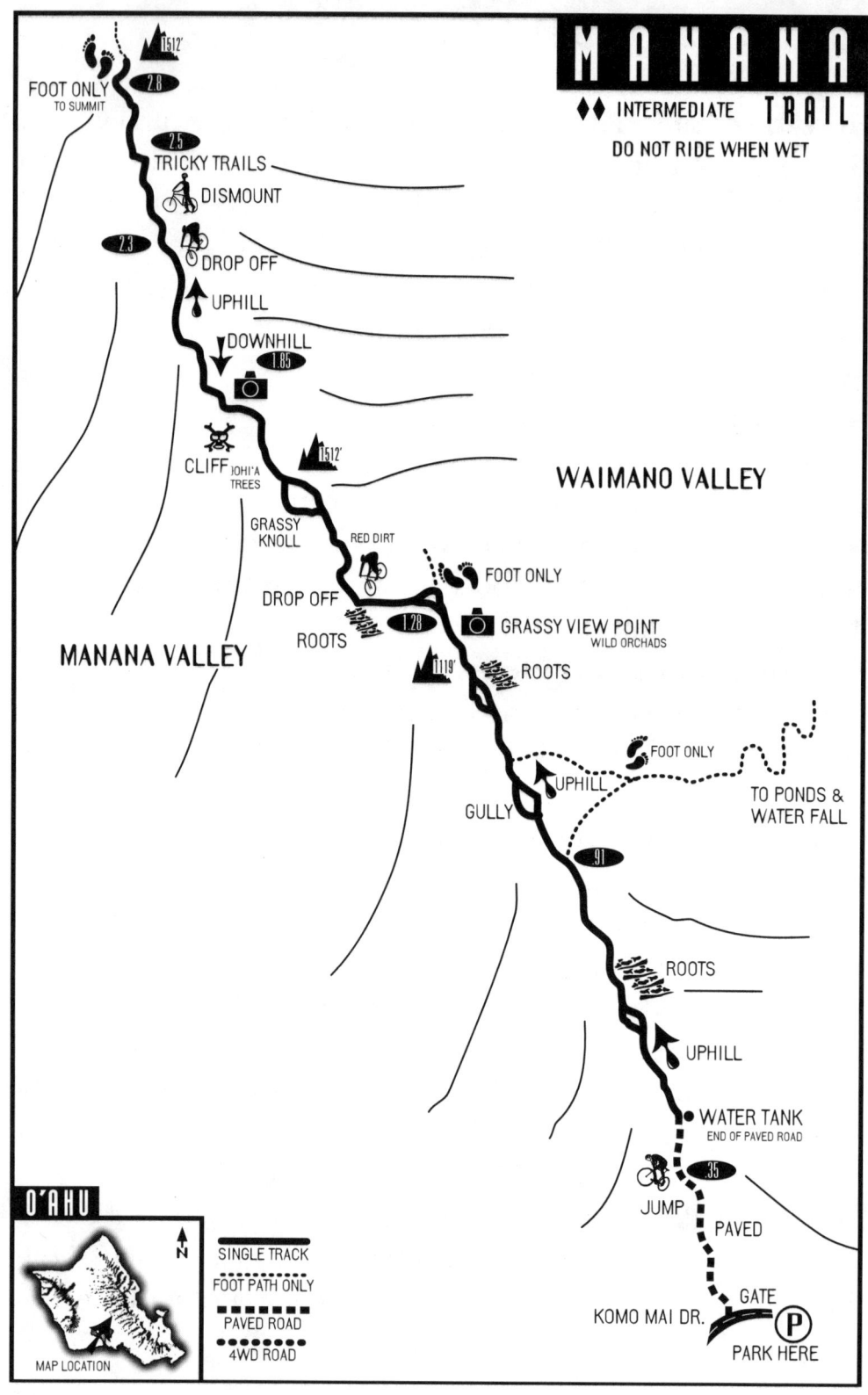

Dropping into the trail again will lead you to some tricky sections that will require dismounts. The trail continues only a short distance before becoming a steep incline for hiking only. The return downhill will lighten up your day with spectacular views and perfect single track. Use caution riding through the blind turns and be courteous to other trail users.

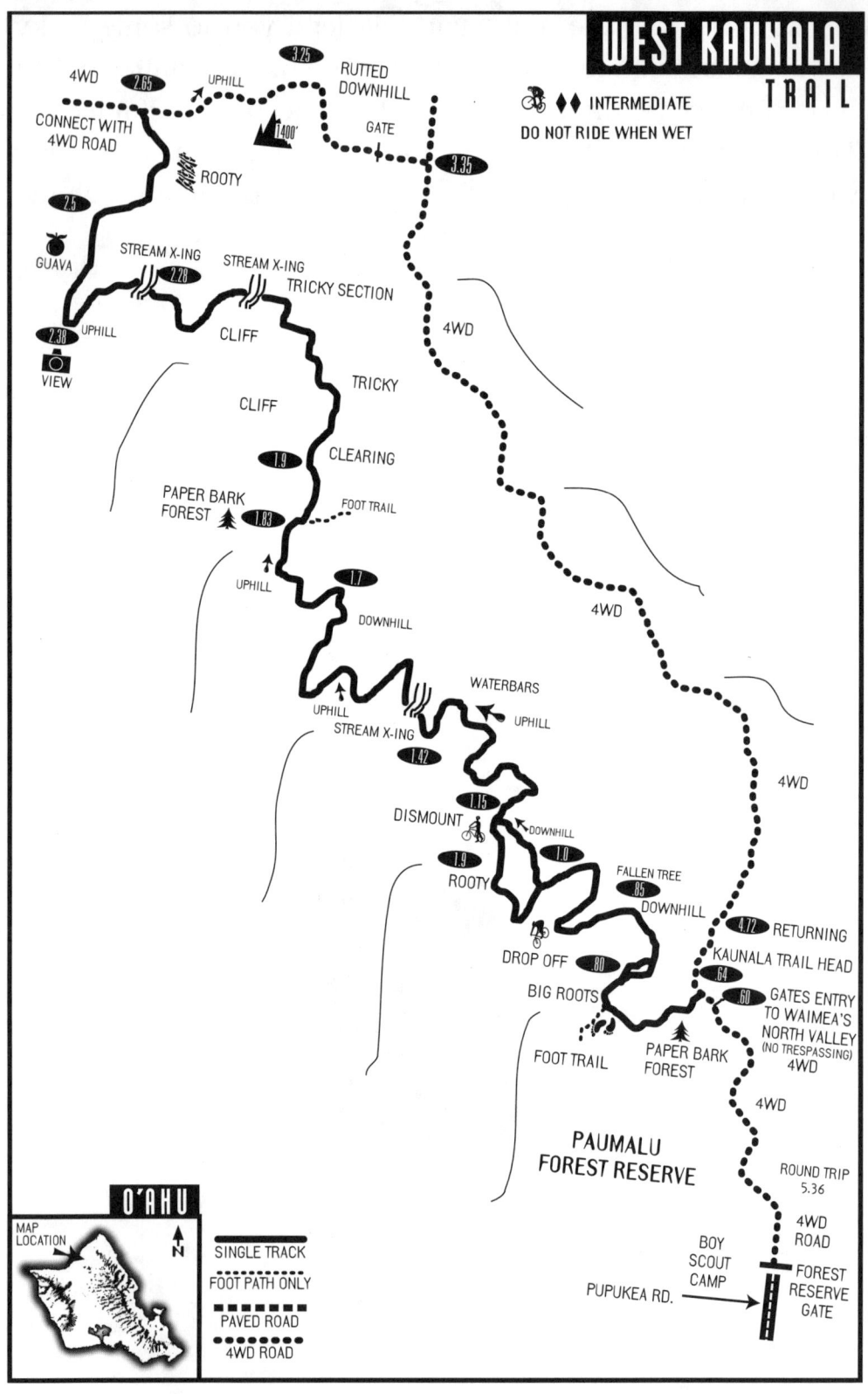

West Kaunala Trail in Pupukea

How to get there: Drive to the North Shore on Kamehameha Hwy 83. Turn mauka on Pupukea Road which is directly across from the Sunset Fire Station. Continue up approx. 2.7 miles until you reach the end of the road and park on the public road outside the Boy Scout Camp. Ride your bike up past the locked Forest Reserve gate and follow the 4WD road approx. .64 mile until you see the Kaunala Trail head on your left.

West Kaunala Trail: 2.65 miles one way
Rating: Intermediate (with dismounts)
Special: No permit is needed. However, access to this trail is allowed only on weekends, state and national holidays. The state shares access with the military. On weekdays, this road may be in use for military training exercises.
Note: Single track and 4WD road. On rainy days, only the access roads should be ridden. DO NOT ride single track when wet or raining. Stay on main trail.
Hazards: Cliffs, roots, rocks, recreational vehicles and hunting.
Amenities: None
Elevation range: 1,400 feet

This awesome trail is the epitome of tropical mountain biking. Follow the dirt road which leads you to the beginning of the single track at the .64 mile mark. This serpentine trail goes down through forests of paper bark trees.

Kaunala has an abundance of protruding roots that range from two inches to one foot in height, making it a bit more technical than the average trail. Kaunala also has downhills which will put your okole (butt) over your rear tire and uphills that will burn your legs. With all the surrounding beauty and tropical splendor, try to stay focused on the trail. There are many steep and hazardous cliff areas throughout this trail. You will see a few small foot trails that go off from the main trail. Some of these are used by hunters and should not be attempted on bike.

You will cross at least three flowing streams and traverse many ridges before reaching the final climb. On your final ascent in "granny gear", you will connect to a 4WD road which will lead you back up to the starting point. You may see motorcycles and 4WD trucks along this dirt road, so use caution. If you hear motorized vehicles approaching, quickly pull to the side of the road and wait until they pass. The dirt road will eventually go down and intersect with another dirt road, just beyond a gate. Turn right at this intersection and follow the road to your original starting position. The roundtrip is approx. 5.36 miles.

Hauʻula Loop Trail

How to get there: Located above Hauʻula Homesteads on Oʻahu's northeast shore. Follow Kamehameha Hwy 83 north past Sacred Falls State Park. Take a left at Hauʻula Homestead Road. When you reach the fork, turn right onto Maʻakua Road. Drive to the end of road and park. Follow the dirt road to the left. Access to the trail head will be on your right.

Hauʻula Loop: 2.9 miles round trip
Rating: Intermediate (with dismounts)
Special: No permit needed. Stay on main trail.
Note: Single track. DO NOT ride when wet or raining.
Hazards: Loose terrain, cliffs, roots, rocks and hunting.
Amenities: Camping by permit only.
History: The Hauʻula Loop trail was cut in 1878.
Elevation range: 700 feet

Hauʻula Loop is an epic single track that zigzags up the right side of the mountain. It crosses over Waipilopilo Gulch and crests the ridge top overlooking beautiful Kaipapaʻu Valley. Hauʻula Loop is a great ride without a lot of bike-carrying. The terrain consists of roots, rocks, a couple of small streams and one swimming hole at the end of your downhill (see map). There are a couple of areas where you may need to dismount. Off-camber and rutted trail sections may be tricky. Use your own judgement and common sense.

A variety of seasonal tropical fruits, such as lilikoi (passion fruit), strawberry guava and guava are found in abundance here. Fantastic views and a flawless downhill single track makes Hauʻula Loop Trail an island treat. Bring a camera and capture your journey on film. The contrast of blue

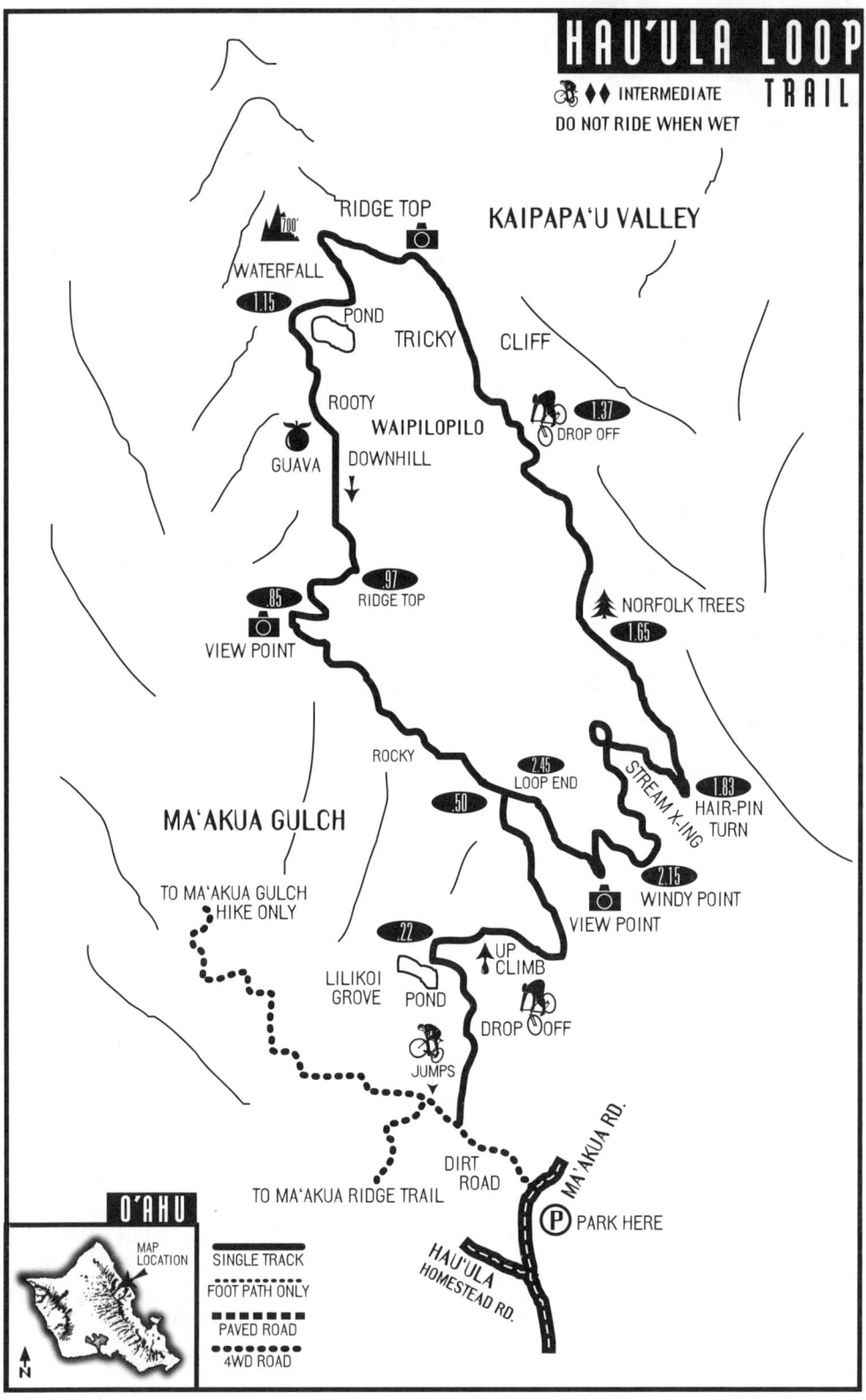

ocean against the dark green mountains make for exceptional photos.

If you still have the energy after the Hau'ula Loop Trail, try the neighboring Ma'akua Ridge Trail. When riding these two trails back to back, you will have spent the day experiencing some of the island's greatest single track.

View of Kaipapa'u Valley from Hau'ula Loop Trail.

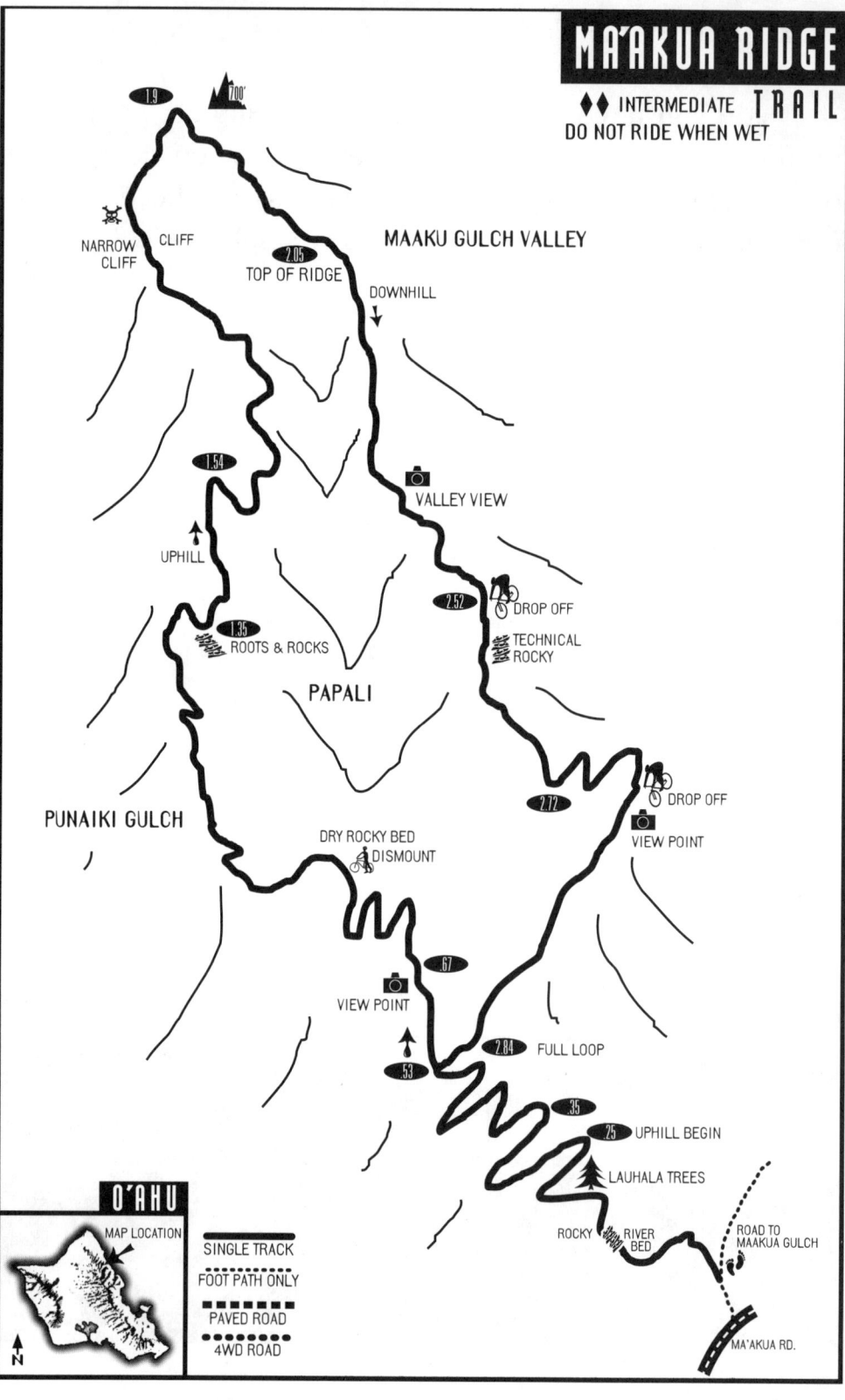

Ma'akua Ridge Trail

How to get there: Located above Hau'ula Homesteads on O'ahu's northeast shore. Follow Kamehameha Hwy 83 north past Sacred Falls State Park. Take a left at Hau'ula Homestead Road. When you reach the fork, turn right onto Ma'akua Road. Drive to end of road and park. Follow the dirt road to the left. Access to the trail head will be on the left just past the Hau'ula Loop Trail.

Ma'akua Ridge Trail: 3.35 miles round-trip
Rating: Intermediate (with dismounts)
Special: No permit needed. Stay on main trail.
Note: Single track. DO NOT ride when wet or raining.
Hazards: Cliffs, narrow and loose terrain, roots, rocks and hunters.
Amenities: None
Elevation range: 700 feet

You will need to carry your bike across a stream bed to reach the other side. This challenging uphill ride begins with a switchback up the left side of Ma'akua Gulch. Some tricky areas are found in various spots along the winding turns. Dismount where appropriate.

This loop trail will bring you back to your original starting position. You will find spectacular views of the northeastern coastline along this trail. An arduous uphill climb traverses the Papali and Punaiki Gulch. This tropical mountain side also has lilikoi and guava fruit which flourish at different times of the year. Endulging in fresh, hand-picked fruit while mountain biking on this Hawaiian trail brings a feeling of tropical paradise.

Once you've reached the final ridge top, you will find the

view of Ma'akua Valley outstanding. Below, the valley whispers. The sound of leaves and branches rustling in the wind, as birds of different color navigate the steep hillside. Truly a wonder of O'ahu, Ma'akua is a must for mountain biking.

Now, get ready for a fun single track downhill. Hikers, cliff areas and some technical areas exist along this narrow trail, so use caution. The trail will connect with itself. At this intersection, hang a left and descend the same switchback to the valley floor. Be careful crossing the stream bed if the water levels are high.

Maunawili Trail

How to get there: Located on Oʻahu's windward side. From Honolulu, take the Pali Hwy 61 through the Pali tunnels. Stay in your right lane and pull off at the first scenic lookout. Park and lock your car. The trail head is located near the scenic lookout entrance.

You may also connect to this trail from the Pali Lookout. Park your car at the lookout and follow the old Pali Road to the right from viewpoint. (see map)

Maunawili Trail: 11 miles one way
Rating: Intermediate (with dismounts)
Special: No permit needed. Stay on main trail. Long distance.
Note: Single track. DO NOT ride if wet or raining.
Hazards: Cliffs, steep grades, loose terrain, roots and rocks. During windy days, the Pali Lookout area sometimes has thousands of bees clinging to the ground for safety. The intersection of the old Pali Hwy Access Trail and the Maunawili Trail has an active beehive.

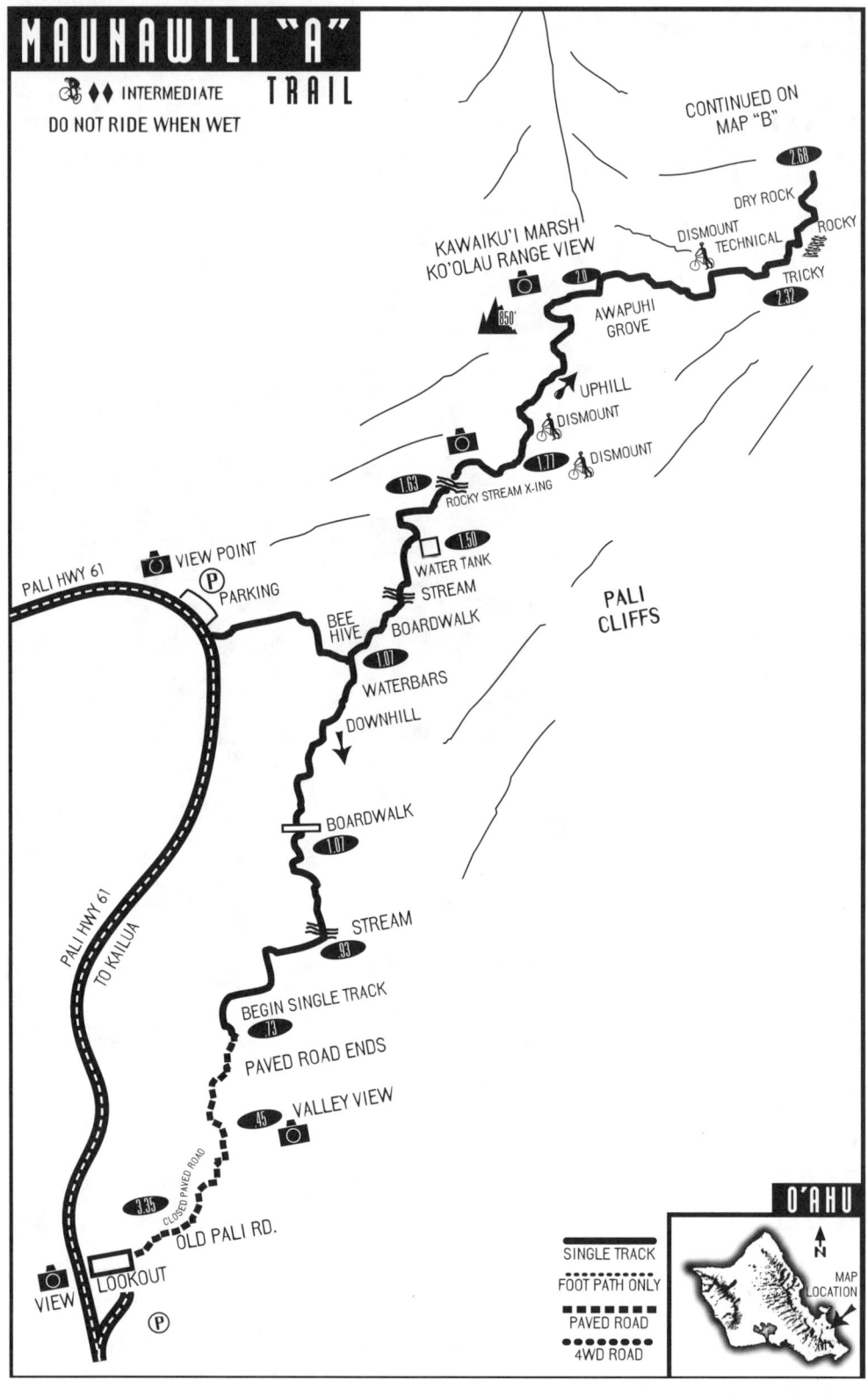

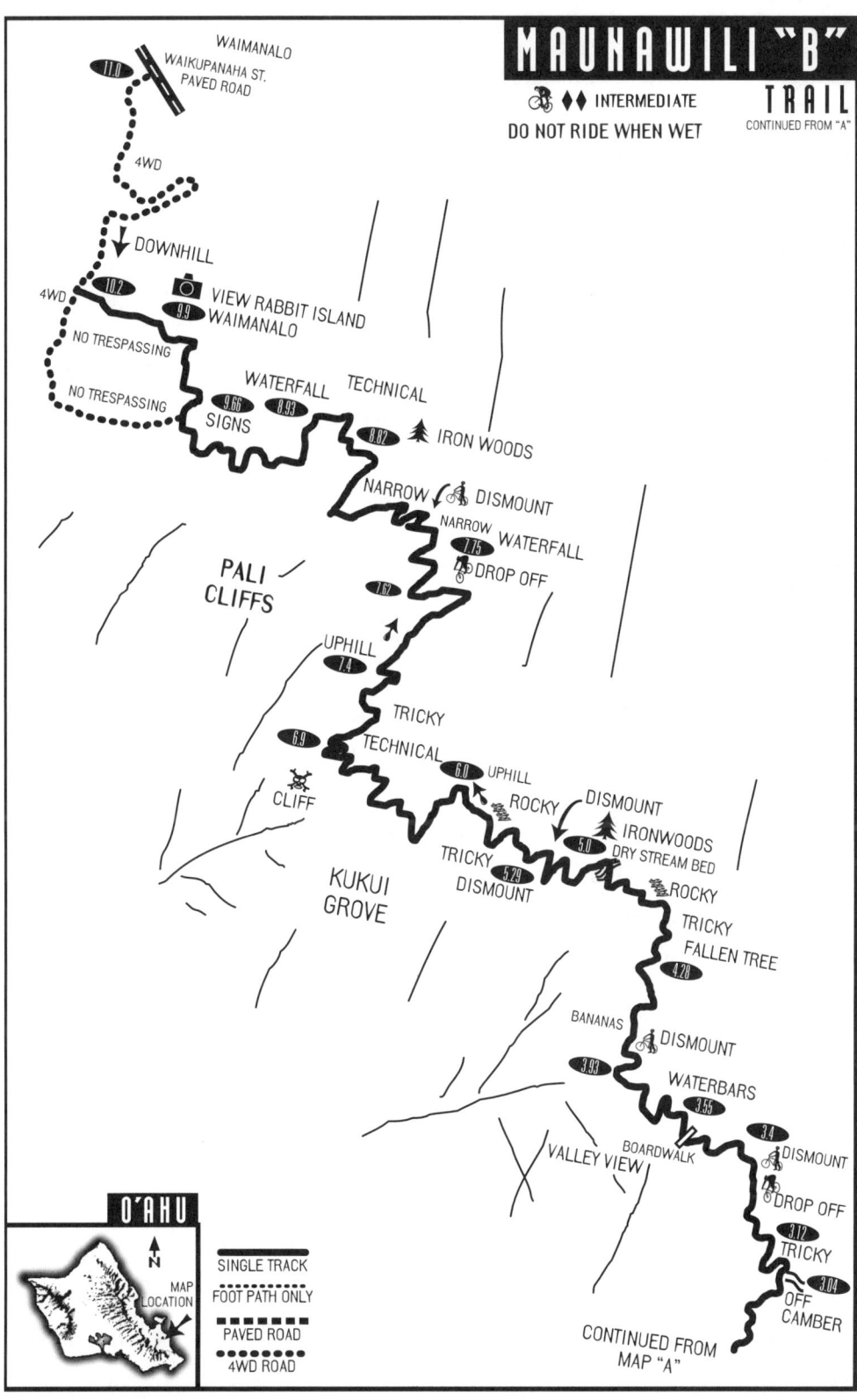

Amenities: Parking

History: Single track cut in 1991 by volunteers and the Sierra Club. The old Pali Highway was built in 1897 and was used by windward and leeward Oʻahu residents as the fastest method of crossing the Koʻolau Mountains.

Elevation range: 800 feet

An exceptional ride. One of Oʻahu's newest trails, Maunawili Trail is already on the verge of being endangered. Often moist, this tropical environment has plenty of overgrown trees which shade the trail and prevent water evaporation. Until reconstruction of these wet areas is finished, riders should avoid all puddled areas by dismounting and walking their bikes.

Situated at the base of the Koʻolau Range, this trail offers the most scenic ride on the island. Winding in and out of numerous little valleys gives you an example of the islands volcanic make-up. As you ride, a variety of sites, sounds, terrains and landscapes make you realize why this trail is so popular with hikers and bikers. The mauka side of the trail harbors steep, intense Pali's (cliffs) and the makai side offers views of Kailua, Olomana and Waimanalo. The blue Pacific is also easy to see in the distance.

Along this 11 mile trail, you will notice a variety of trail restoration efforts made by various volunteer groups and Na Ala Hele. Water-bars, log steps and boardwalks have been constructed to help minimize impact to the soft and moist trail below. Throughout the trail, many puddled areas are found. Riders should dismount and walk your bike when passing these fragile sections of trail.

This is an out and back trail. Starting the Maunawili Trail at the Pali Hwy and ending in Waimanalo, round trip totals 22 miles. Be prepared for a few hours on the trail. If you don't have a car waiting for you at the Waimanalo end, remember, it's a long trip, so bring plenty of snacks and water. Don't forget your camera.

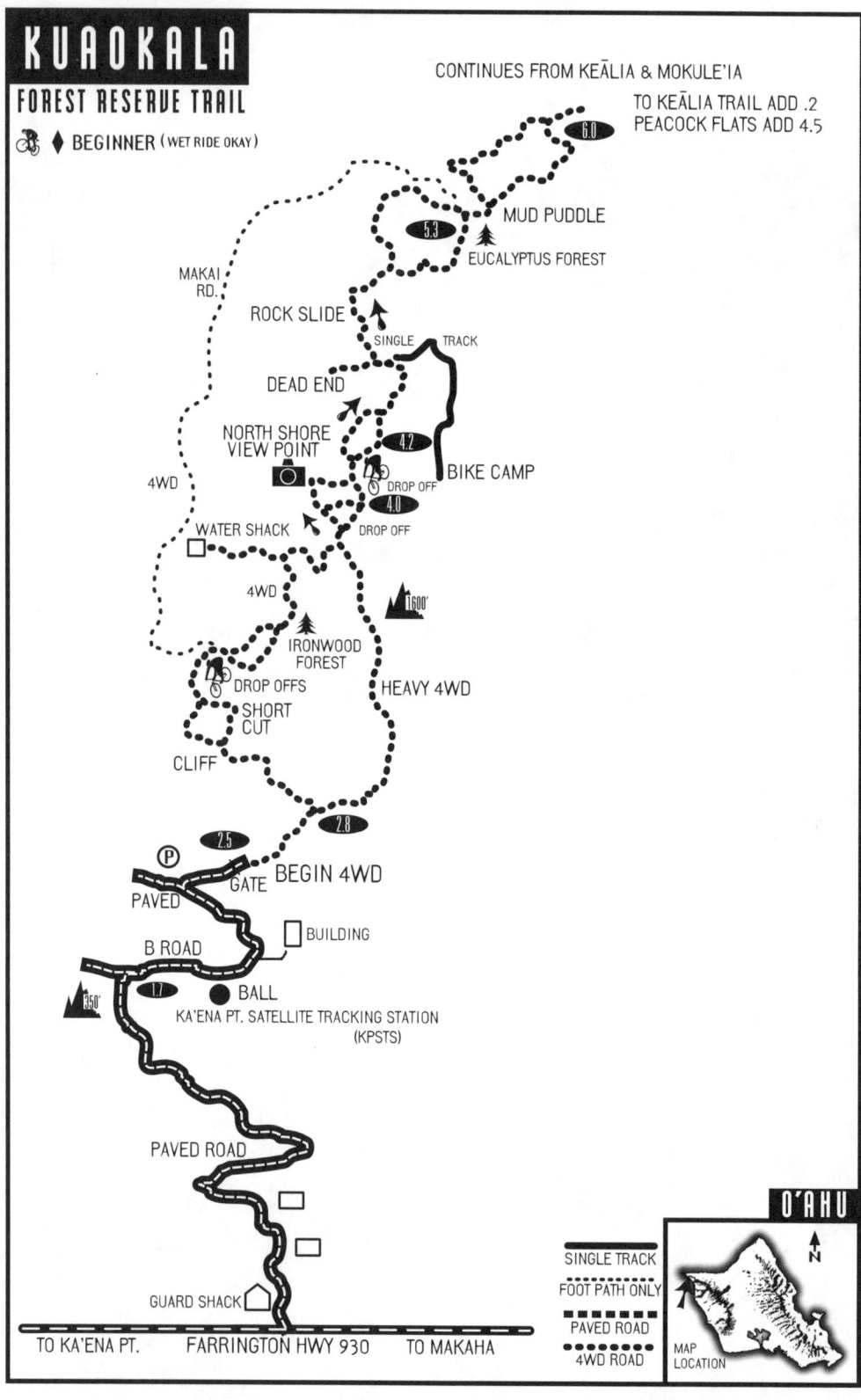

KUAOKALA FOREST RESERVE TRAIL
(VIA KA'ENA POINT SATELLITE TRACKING STATION {KPSTS})

How to get there: Located at the western tip of O'ahu's Wai'anae Range. Follow Farrington Hwy 930 westbound past Wai'anae until you reach Keawa'ula or Yokohama Beach. Turn right and follow the Ka'ena Point Satellite Tracking Station (KPSTS) access road. You are required to stop at the guard shack to furnish valid I.D. and a permit from DLNR. See Permit Information.

Kuaokala via KPSTS: 10.5 miles one way to Peacock Flats.
Rating: Beginner (with dismounts)
Special: A permit is needed to enter and exit via the KPSTS or when camping at Peacock Flats campground. See Permit Information.
Note: First 2.5 miles is paved. Then 7.0 miles of 4WD road. Wet riding ok.
Hazards: 4WD's, hunters, cliff areas. Road is slippery when wet.
Amenities: Parking, camping, portable restroom and shelter at Peacock Flats.
Elevation range: 1,400 feet

The Kuaokala Forest Reserve offers great biking for all riding abilities. Riders can park their car at the parking area just before dropping down the hill from B Road. (See map)

For experienced riders, the roads offer a challenging complex of detours, short cuts and alternate routes. Go fast, ride hard, and enjoy the mountain scenery against the blue Pacific. Remember, other bikers and hikers, as well as 4WD trucks use these roads, so use caution and travel at speeds that are safe.

Beginner mountain bikers will find miles of 4WD roads that provide a relatively safe trip, due to its wide roads. Typical bumpy terrain with uphills and downhills give beginners a good sense of mauka trail riding. The more conservative riders can just follow the main road indicated by the arrow signs. Use your odometer and map to determine mileage and alternate routes.

Kuaokala is a long ride, and riders should prepare for a few hours minimum when riding out and back. No water is available on this long journey, so bring plenty with you.

The Makai Road is a 7 mile 4WD road that parallels the main road. It is less traveled and has deep mud puddles under its overgrown trees. Always a fun ride, it is makai (oceanside) of the main road and travels through cool forests full of tropical birds.

The roads fork in different directions, so follow your map. The Kealia Trail links with the main road and is the only single track for mountain bikes in this area. To access this advanced route, see the Kealia Trail map.

The dirt road will eventually intersect with a paved access road that comes up from Mokule'ia (see Mokule'ia map). Take a left and follow the paved road down and up to a locked gate. Peacock Flats campground is on your immediate right. A sheltered picnic table and one portable restroom is available for use. Camping is allowed by permit only.

Mokuleʻia Access Road to Peacock Flats

How to get there: The Mokuleʻia Access Road is located on Oʻahu's scenic northwestern coast. Head north on Farrington Hwy 930. Drive past Waialua High School and continue for two miles until you reach the first left at the coconut tree farm. Park on the right as you enter the access road. Do not leave valuables in the car which might provoke thieves.

As you proceed up this road, you will pass three gates which are usually locked. If they are open, do not attempt to drive a vehicle past them or your vehicle may be locked in.

Mokuleʻia Access to Peacock Flats: 3.8 miles one way
Rating: Intermediate
Special: No permit is necessary to use this access road. Camping at Peacock Flats or exiting via the Kaʻena Point Satellite Tracking Station road will require a permit from DLNR. See Permit Information.
Note: Paved road. Wet ride ok. The Pahole Reserve is a Natural Area Reserves System (NARS). No bikes on single track (see map).
Hazards: Livestock, occasional vehicular traffic and cliff areas.
Amenities: Camping, portable restroom and shelter.
Elevation range: 1,200 feet

Start this ride in the cool of the morning or late afternoon as there is minimal shade. Bring plenty of water, sunscreen and a hat to protect yourself from the sun and heat. The Mokuleʻia Access Road is a paved road which travels up an arduous incline. If you can conquer this hill without a dismount, you are ready for anything.

The first mile from the parking lot is level with a mild

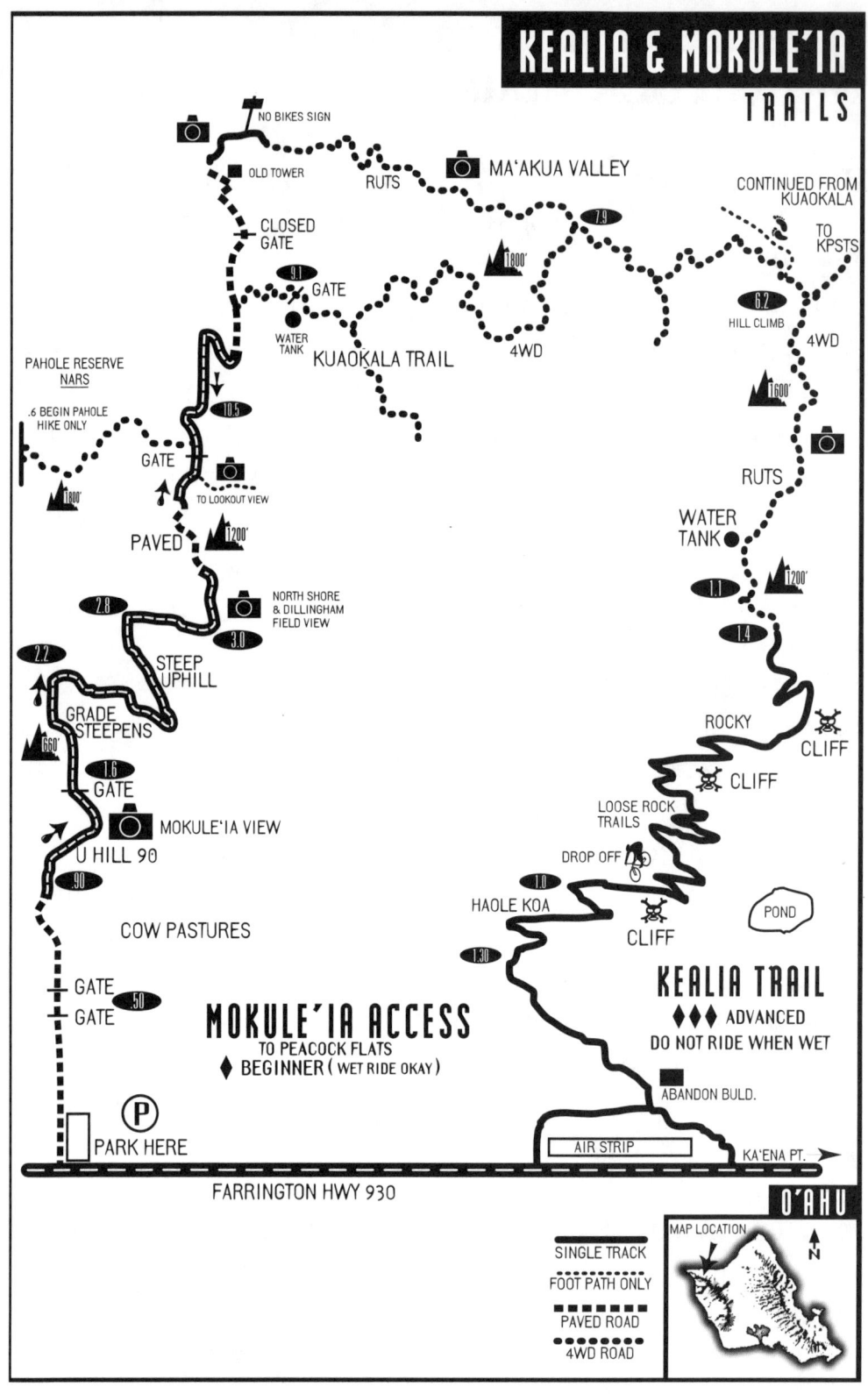

uphill. At the 2.2 mile mark, the uphill grade steepens, and riding becomes very slow and hot as it passes through cow pastures. If the physical demands of this ride don't take your breath away, the spectacular views of the North Shore certainly will. During the winter months from November to May, you may be able to see humpback whales off-shore.

Peacock Flats campground will be on your left just past the last gate approx. 3.8 miles. You may follow the 4WD road on the left up another .5 mile to the Pahole Reserve boundary. Being a Natural Area Reserves System, the hiking trail is off-limits to mountain bikes. If you leave your bike behind, the hike will take you to breathtaking view of Makua Valley on Oʻahu's western shoreline.

Follow the paved road another .80 mile to access the Kuaokala 4WD road. This connects to the Kealia Trail and the Kaʻena Point Satellite Tracking Station. (see map)

Kealia Trail

How to get there: This technical trail is located above Dillingham Airfield in Mokuleʻia on Oʻahu's northwest coast. The Kealia Trail has a steep grade with loose terrain, so it is not ridable as an uphill.

This trail can be accessed in two different ways. For directions to connect to the Kealia Trail from above, refer to the map of Mokuleʻia Access to Peacock Flats or Kuaokala F.R. Road (KPSTS).

Kealia Trail: 2.8 miles one way (Not including access routes. Add mileage from Peacock Flats or KPSTS)
Rating: Advanced (with dismounts)
Special: No permit needed when accessed from the Mokuleʻia

Access Road. Permit only needed when using the KPSTS access. See Permit Information.

Note: 4WD and single track. DO NOT RIDE single track on wet or rainy days.

Hazards: Steep cliffs, loose and narrow terrain, roots and rocks.

Amenities: None

Elevation range: 1,600 feet

The Kealia Trail is a fun and technical downhill ride. At about the .75 mark of the 4WD road, certain areas are rutted out due to rain and erosion. Be careful if you are going fast. Follow the signs when the road forks or check your map. At the end of the road you will find the beginning of the single track on your left, hidden in the ironwood forest. Now is the time to adjust those shocks and put them to the test. The next 1.35 miles is a bumpy switchback that harbors steep cliffs with loose rocks, drop-offs and various technical terrain. Use extreme caution and dismount when appropriate.

Only competent advanced mountain bikers should challenge this trail.

This trail offers some fantastic views of the North Shore and Mokule'ia. Directly below the trail lies the Dillingham Airfield. This is the home of glider rides, aerobatic bi-planes and skydiving schools. While on the trail, you can sometimes see and hear the sailplanes flying low overhead. Sometimes, they fly so close, you can see their smiling faces.

Just off-shore, surfers ride waves during the winter season. The waves on this northern coastline get as big as 20 to 30 feet. Only a brave few ever take that challenge.

When you reach the bottom of the trail, you will pass the glider port. You may turn left at Farrington Hwy 930 to Ka'ena Point or go right to the Mokule'ia Access Road.

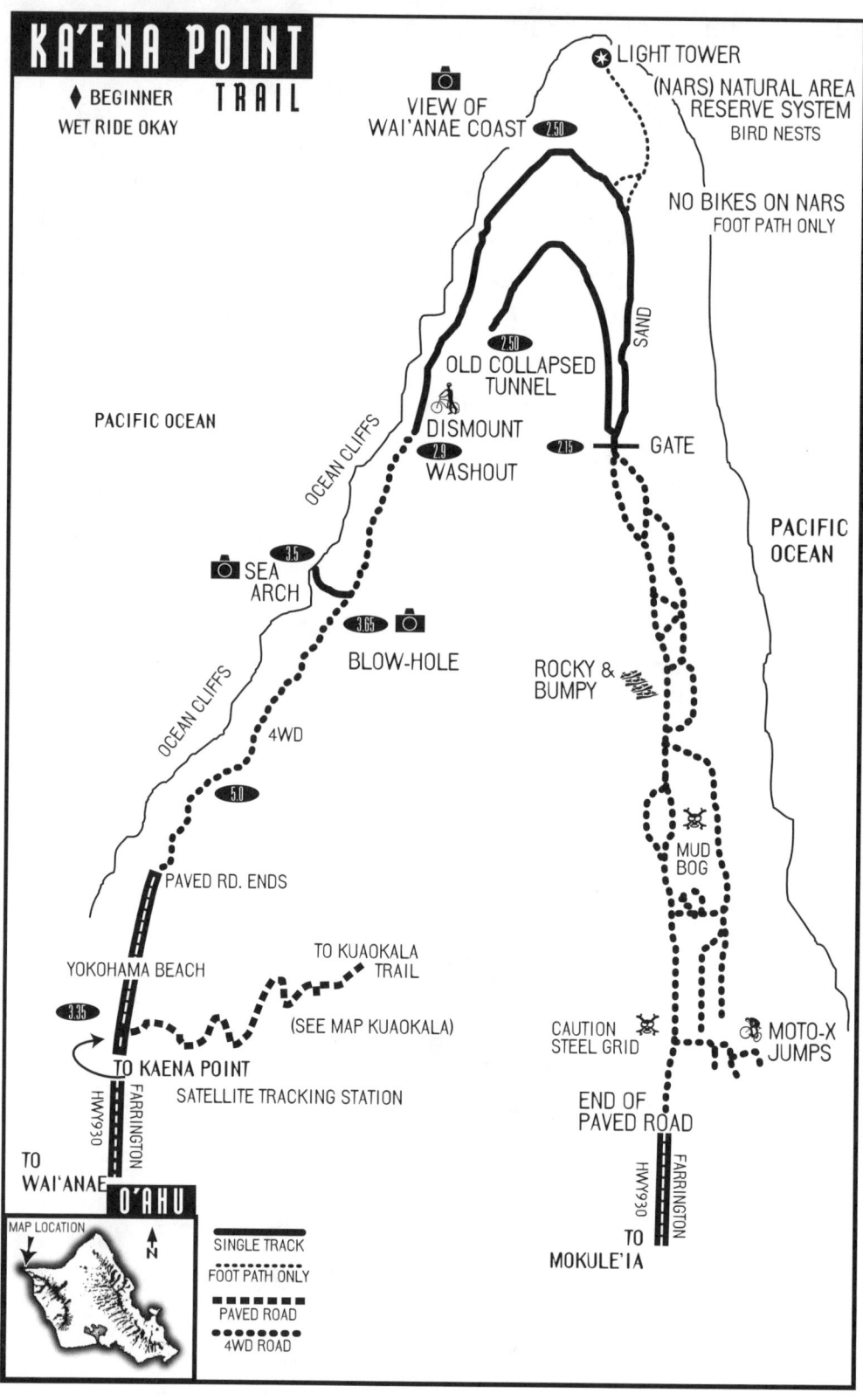

Ka'ena Point Trail

How to get there: Located at the westernmost tip of O'ahu. Head west on Farrington Hwy 930 in Mokule'ia to the end of the paved road. Park and lock your car, but do not leave valuables in the car.

Ka'ena Point: 5.0 miles one way
Rating: Beginner (with dismounts)
Special: No permit is needed to enter the Ka'ena Point area. The roads and dunes near the lighthouse are part of a Natural Area Reserves System NARS. This fragile coastal ecosystem consists of many endangered native Hawaiian plants and animals. Be extremely careful when entering into this area. Absolutely no bikes are allowed in the bird nesting area, as bikes frighten the nesting seabirds. Leave your bike outside the walking path (see map), and only enter on foot to view this native coastal ecosystem. Stay on the main trail. No pets allowed.
Note: 4WD road. Wet ride ok, however, beware of the clay-like mud which is hard to ride.
Hazards: The winter months bring dangerous high surf, so stay clear of areas exposed to breaking waves.
Watch out for motorcycles, 4WD's, ATV's and hikers.
Amenities: Showers and restrooms at Yokohama Beach Park
History: Also known as leina a ka'uhane, the "leaping place of souls". In ancient times, Hawaiians believed that souls of the dead leap off an area of this point into the land of dead.

An old railroad track, still visible in some areas, is from a time when trains were used to transport pineapple around the point.
Elevation range: Ocean level

It is recommended that you start this ride in the cool of the morning or late afternoon as there is very minimal shade. Bring plenty of water, sunscreen and a hat to protect yourself from the sun and heat.

Ka'ena is a visitors paradise and is known for its dry and beautiful setting along the blue Pacific. This semi-level bumpy road goes around the entire point and ends at Yokohama Beach.

As seen on your map, the Mokule'ia side of the point is a maze of dirt roads. The mauka road consists mainly of dirt and rock, while the makai road is mostly sand. If you are caught in the rain on this ride, try to take the makai road because it is more porous. The clay-like mud of the mauka road will quickly cake-up your tires and prevent tire rotation.

Beyond the gated boulder barricade lies the NARS. The clearly marked main trail will bring you around the point without disturbing this fragile ecosystem. If you want to view the protected area, keep your bike outside on the main trail and walk in via the sandy path. Stay on the main trail. The Laysan albatross' and the wedge-tailed shearwaters have their nesting grounds here, so don't take short-cuts or make your own path.

During the winter breeding season, generally November through May, Humpback whales are often seen breaching off the point. The endangered Hawaiian monk seals can also be sighted resting on the beaches. Only an estimated 1000 are still surviving today. Take all the pictures you desire, but do not disturb the wildlife by getting to close. Terns, red footed boobies, green sea turtles and spinner dolphins can sometimes be seen from this dry, wind-swept point.

Towards the Yokohama side, there is one area where the sea has completely eroded the trail, so be careful. You will need to dismount and carefully carry your bike across to continue.

Continue further and look for the small blow hole in the rocks on the right side. Follow the kiawe tree laced road a short distance to the end at Yokohama Beach. Showers and restrooms are available across from the beach. High surf and hidden reef are common at this beach, so use caution if swimming here.

7 Private Lands

Some of the most incredible places to ride on Oʻahu are on private property. For this reason, detailed maps of these areas are not provided. Authorized access is required for your safety. If you choose to ride on private property, it is your responsibility to get permission and to obey their rules. Security personnel patrol these areas and can have you arrested for trespassing.

Mililani

How to get there: Head north on the H-2 freeway. Take the Ka Uka Blvd. exit #2 and turn right. Follow road down the Panaikauahi Gulch and back up the other side. Turn at the first right at the Waiawa Correctional Facility sign and proceed up the hill approximately 1.5 miles. Off the paved road, many dirt roads and trails disappear into the woods. Park on public roads and follow any of these for access to the riding trails.

Rating: Intermediate (with dismounts)

Special: Permission is only granted to organized groups and clubs that provide releases and carry insurance. Contact Gentry Properties and Castle & Cooke Land Company. See

Appendix for contact number.
Note: Wet ride ok. May be slippery and/or cake-like mud.
Amenities: None
Hazards: Recreational vehicles, roots, rocks, cliff areas and loose terrain.

Mililani has miles of 4WD roads and single tracks and is often used by 4WD's, motorcycles and ATV's. Use caution when you hear approaching motorized vehicles. Pull well off the road or trail and wait for them to pass.

You can ride for hours here and never see your own tracks. Mililani has seemingly endless single tracks and dirt roads. Remember where you came from so you don't get lost.

An all day ride will take you past incredible scenery and different terrain. Roots, rocks, and overgrown trees and bushes make Mililani a real challenge. Uphill leg burns and fast downhills, mixed with winding turns and tricky stream crossings are also common. A variety of tropical fruit can be found throughout your ride. Bring plenty of water and energy food. You'll definitely need it.

Kahuku

How to get there: Head north on Kam Hwy on O'ahu's North Shore. Pass the Sunset Beach Elementary School approximately 1.2 miles. On the mauka side of the highway, you will see a dirt road for the Kahuku Moto-X Track. Follow the dirt road up to the gate. Here you will need to pay an entry fee. Continue up the road until you reach the race track. Park your vehicle and beware of motorcycles.

Rating: Beginner to advanced
Special: Permit is not needed. However, a $5.00 fee per bike

per day is required. Park is open from 8am-6pm weekends and federal holidays only.

Note: 4WD road and single track. Wet ride ok. May be slippery and have cake-like mud.

Amenities: Camping and portable restrooms.

Hazards: Motorcycles, 4WD's, ATV's, cliffs, roots, rocks and loose terrain.

Located on Oʻahu's scenic North Shore. The Kahuku Race Track is on state land that is leased by Hawaiʻi Motorsports Association. The track is primarily used for motorcycle racing and practice sessions on weekends and federal holidays. Mountain bikers should stay off the race track. Ride on the many 4WD roads and single tracks that comprise the Kahuku area. Yield to motorcycles at all times. Strict regulations regarding helmet use apply. DO NOT be caught with out your helmet on, or you will be asked to leave.

When you ride Kahuku, you are blessed with miles of perfect mountain bike roads and trails. Steep uphills and fast downhills with plenty of technical riding for trials riders. The forests consist of ironwood trees with dry twigs covering the ground. Be ready for fast and furious riding. Kahuku is a great ride for aggressive riders who just have to skid, slide and make shortcuts. Once you visit Kahuku, rest assured, you'll be back. See Appendix for contact number.

Queen's Beach

How to get there: Proceed east on Kalanianaʻole Highway 72. Pass Sandy Beach Park approximately 1.5 miles. On the makai side of the road there is an undeveloped section of land opposite the Hawaiʻi Kai Golf Course. Park on the public roads well off the highway.

Rating: Beginner (with dismounts)
Special: Permission is needed from the owner Bishop Estate or their lessee. See Appendix.
Note: 4WD and single track area. Wet ride ok. Prepare for hot and dry climate with minimal shade.
Amenities: Parking, swimming and fishing.
Hazards: Surf, rocky shoreline, loose terrain and recreational vehicles.
History: Former ranch land of Alan Davis. The Davis home was destroyed by a devastating tsunami in 1946. Some remnants may still exist.
Elevation range: Ocean level

This entire area is private property and owned by Bishop Estate. It offers approximately 20 acres of non-developed coastal property with perfect trails for beginner mountain bikers. The trails also provide a good test for your suspension. The terrain consists of rocks, boulders, Whoop-D-Doos and a combination of dried dirt, wet mud and deep sand roads.

Fronting this land is a beautiful coastline. High surf is common along this shoreline, predominately during the summer. Use caution when riding near shoreline or when swimming. Queen's Beach bakes in the sun, so bring plenty of water and sunscreen. Certain areas may require a dismount because of steep drop-offs or loose gravel.

8 Guided Tours

In Hawai'i, several clubs offer organized rides that cater to mountain bikers with all levels of experience. Some of the rides are free and others on private property, may include a fee. To find out more about group rides, contact the listed clubs. See Mountain Bike Clubs for contact numbers.

If you're looking for a guided mountain bike tour through hidden Hawai'i, then the following is for you. Some of the best rides are found on private property which is only accessed by permission or on a guided tour. Two particular guided tours that offer incredible landscape, history, and rented bikes and helmets are the Kualoa Ranch Adventures and the Waimea Valley Adventures.

Kualoa Ranch

Hot to get there: Located on northeastern coast of O'ahu. From Honolulu, drive north on H-1 and take the Likelike Hwy. (63) over the Ko'olau Range to the windward side. Go north at Kahekili Hwy 83 and it will merge with Kamehameha Hwy 830. Drive the scenic route until you see the entrance to Kualoa Ranch directly across from the Kualoa Regional Beach Park. Obtain permission through the Kualoa Ranch Office. Call in advance to arrange for group tours or private rides.

Kualoa Ranch's Pilali Valley tour: 3.0 miles round trip
Rating: Beginner
Special: Each activity may require separate fees. Inquire with

ranch activity desk. Bikes and helmets provided. See Appendix for phone number.

Note: 4WD and single track. Wet ride ok.

Hazards: Some loose terrain and steep grades exist. May be slippery when wet.

Amenities: Parking, restaurants, water, restrooms and phones.

This is a one hour adventure that starts at the ranch office. Your tour-guide will take you on a dirt road that passes through three gates and several cattle pastures. You will meet some of the ranch's prized livestock. Then it's a steady but gradual climb to several hundred feet above sea level.

When you reach the 1.5 mile mark, the ride ends and the short hike begins. This usually damp trail climbs up another hundred feet through beautiful groves of tropical fruit. Lilikoi (passion fruit) and strawberry guava are ripe several times during the year. It's a real pleasure picking fresh island fruit as you hike. The trail comes out of the cool, shaded forest and ends at a clearing which looks out over Kaneohe Bay. To your right side is the awesome Hakipu'u Valley. From here, the famous Chinaman's Hat or Mokoli'i Island sits just offshore. In the distance, you can see the Kaneohe Bay sandbar which is dry land during low tide and completely underwater at high tide. The sandbar is a great place for parties and barbeques when it's exposed.

Ka'a'awa Valley tour: 4.0 miles one way
Rating: Beginner
Special: Customized single track tours available upon request. Activity fees may vary. See Appendix for contact numbers and further information. Bikes and helmets are provided, but you can bring your own.

Note: 4WD road and single track. Wet ride ok.
Hazards: Some loose terrain and steep grades. May be slippery when wet.
Amenities: Parking, restaurants, water, restrooms and phones.

This 4,000 acre ranch is one of the preferred sites for local mountain bike competitions. It was also one of the locations for the first Hawaiian Mountain Bike Pro/Am in 1995. Kualoa Ranch includes the 1,000 acre Ka'a'awa Valley. Famous for its backdrop in "Jurassic Park" and televisions short lived "Birds of Paradise", Ka'a'awa Valley is the same valley in which your guided tour will include a bike, helmet, complimentary water bottle and finally, a barbeque lunch when you're pau (finished).

Whether you're an amateur biker or a skilled veteran, you'll be sure to experience the same awesome pleasure of this valley tour. Ride through four miles of pristine tropical valley while your guide gives you a history of the ranch. Cross a

refreshing stream and stop to smell the flowers. Seasonal guava and lilikoi fruit are yours for the picking. As you pass through two gates in the valley, you will find cows grazing in the pastures.

Part of this tour will also include a brief 15 minute hike to a scenic overlook of Kaneohe Bay and Hakipuʻu Valley. As you gaze into the vast blue Pacific, you'll notice the small island of Mokoliʻi just offshore. Commonly known as Chinaman's Hat, legend has it that the goddess Hiʻiaka turned a dragon into stone and what you see is the tip of its tail protruding above the surface of the ocean. Also nearby is the ranch's own private beach which offers snorkeling, volleyball, catamaran, jet skiing and windsurfing.

Kualoa Ranch at a glance: When you want a day of outdoor adventure, Kualoa should at the top of your list. Kualoa has something for everyone, especially the outdoor enthusiast. Choose from mountain biking, hiking, ATV rides and horseback riding. You can also watch Hawaiian cowboys (paniolo) rope cattle or you can take in a breath taking helicopter tour.

If you want ocean activities, Kualoa has it too. Enjoy windsurfing, snorkeling, scuba diving, sailing, canoe paddling, swimming and beach sports like volleyball and badminton. All of this and a delicious Hawaiian style outdoor barbeque. Call Kualoa Ranch and discover what Hawaiʻi is all about.

Waimea Valley

How to get there: Located on the North Shore. From Haleʻiwa town, follow Kamehameha Hwy 83 heading north until you reach Waimea Bay. Turn right after you cross the Waimea River and proceed to Waimea Falls Park. Park near the restaurants.
Waimea's North Valley Tour: approx. 3.0 miles one way

Rating: Beginner or Advanced

Special: Activity fees vary. Inquire within. Bikes and helmets provided, but you can provide your own. See Appendix for contact number.

Hazards: Some loose terrain and steep grades exist. May be slippery when wet.

Amenities: Parking, restaurants, water, restrooms and phones.

Waimea Valley was also one of the sites of the Hawaiian Mountain Tour Pro/Am in 1995. You will ride on the same road that was used in this exciting downhill event.

If you are looking for a "Tour De Hawai'i," perhaps the guided mountain bike tour through the 1800 acre Waimea Valley will satisfy you. Two trails are offered to beginners and advanced riders. A van will take you and your bike to the top (approx 700 feet) of Pupukea Heights above the valley. Your friendly and knowledgeable guide will then lead you on a two hour adventure. You'll descend the north valley on a dirt road while experiencing the scenic ancient lands of Hawai'i. Quench your thirst with island fruit picked fresh from the trees (seasonal) as you ride. This valley has guavas bigger then softballs.

Just when you need it most, you'll pedal through a multitude of refreshing streams to cool you off. Your tour guide will assist you if you need help crossing the stream. Near the finish, a brief 15 minute hike up to a scenic plateau will bring you back to days of old. Look out over the pool at the base of Waimea Valley's waterfall and imagine the time when only native Hawaiians inhabited this pristine land.

Waimea Valley at a glance: After your adventure, take advantage of the rest of what the park has to offer. ATV rides and kayak adventures are among the rest of the activities. If you want to learn more about Hawaiian culture, proceed to the south valley for an experience you'll never forget.

Learn about the endangered native Hawaiian plants and wildlife. Play Hawaiian games and explore the kauhale (ancient living sites). See the evolution of the hula and learn some authentic kahiko dancing moves. At the back of the valley, you can watch professional cliff divers as they plunge from high atop Waimea Falls into the natural pool below. Bring your swimsuit and enjoy the refreshing pool in this tropical wonderland. Contact Waimea Valley Adventures for more information.

A pro rider jumps during the Hawaiian Mountain Tour Pro/Am. Twain Newhart photo.

Appendix

Permit Information

Department of Land and Natural Resources
Division of Forestry and Wildlife (808) 587-0058
888 Mililani Street #700
Honolulu, Hawai'i 96813
* Na Ala Hele - statewide trail and access program
* Natural Area Reserves System (NARS) Information
  native Hawaiian plant and animal protection

Department of Land and Natural Resources
Division of Forestry and Wildlife (808) 587-0166
1151 Punchbowl #325
Honolulu, Hawai'i 96813
* Ka'ena Point Satellite Tracking Station access road (KPSTS)
* camping and picnic permits to Peacock Flats

Hawai'i State Parks (808) 587-0300
1151 Punchbowl Street #310
Honolulu, Hawai'i 96813
* camping and picnic permits for state parks

City & County of Honolulu (808) 523-4525
Dept. of Parks and Recreation
650 S. King St. Ground floor
Honolulu, Hawai'i 96813
* camping and picnic permits for county parks

Private Property Access Contacts

Gentry Properties (808) 599-8366
* Mililani (Waiawa/Waipio)

Castle and Cooke Land Company (808) 548-4811
* Mililani

Hawai'i Motorsports Assn. race info. (808) 239-BIKE
P.O. Box 1654
Honolulu, Hawai'i 96806
* Kahuku motor-cross track

Bishop Estate (808) 523-6200
or Kaiser Chemical Corp. (510) 271-6155
* Queens Beach area

Mountain Bike Tours

Kualoa Ranch Adventures (808) 237-7321 see article
49-560 Kamehameha Hwy. Ka'a'awa, Hawai'i 96730

Waimea Valley Adventures (808) 638-8511 see article
59-864 Kamehameha Hwy. Hale'iwa, Hawai'i 96712

Bike Shops

Bikefactory Sportshop (808) 946-8927
1695 Kapi'olani Blvd.
Honolulu
* sales & service
* rentals

The Bike Way (808) 591-8817
250 Ward Avenue
Honolulu
* sales & service

The Bike Shop (808) 596-0588
Honolulu/Hawai'i Kai/Pearl City/Kaneohe
* sales & service

Island Triathlon and Bike (808) 732-7227
569 Kapahulu Ave.
Honolulu/Hickam/Schofield
* sales & service
* rentals

Hawaiian Island Creations Bike and Surf (808) 266-6730
354 Hahani St.
Kailua/Pearlridge
* sales/service

Raging Isle Sports (808) 637-7707
66-250 Kam. Hwy. Bldg. B
Hale'iwa (North Shore)
* sales & service
* rentals

Fantasy Cycles (808) 637-3221
66-134 Kam. Hwy.
Hale'iwa (North Shore)
* sales/service/rentals

Eki Cyclery (808) 847-2005
1603 Dillingham Blvd.

Honolulu
* sales/service

McCully Bike Shop (808) 955-6329
2124 S. King St.
Honolulu
* sales/service

SportsNut (808) 488-6844
Times Square Shopping Center
* sales/service

Waipahu Bicycle and Sporting Goods (808) 671-4091
94-320 Waipahu Depot
* sales/service

Mountain Bike Rentals

Island Triathlon and Bike (808) 732-7227
Raging Isle Sports (808) 637-7707
Fantasy Cycles (808) 637-3221
Coconut Cruisers (808) 924-1644
Blue Sky Rentals (808) 947-0101
Wiki Wiki Wheels (808) 923-5544

Bike Clubs and Environmental Groups

Hawai'i Bicycling League HBL
John Mathias (808) 735-5756
* group rides on/off road
* trail restoration

* bike education

O'ahu Off-Road Cycling Club
contact The Bike Way at (808) 591-8817
* group rides
* trail restoration

National Off-Road Bicycling Association
NORBA Representative
John Farrar (808) 263-3435
* race promoter & organizer

Sierra Club Hawai'i Chapter
Box 2577
Honolulu, Hawai'i 96803 (808) 538-6616
* hikes
* trail clearing and construction

Hawaiian Trail & Mountain Club
PO Box 2238
Honolulu, Hawai'i 96804 (808) 262-2845
* hikes
* camping
* trail maintenance

Hawai'i Nature Center
2131 Makiki Heights Dr.
Honolulu, Hawai'i 96822 (808) 955-0100
* environmental education for kids
* guided interpretive hikes
* adult classes

The Nature Conservancy

1116 Smith St.#201
Honolulu, Hawai'i 96817 (808) 537-4508
* land & environmental protection
* hikes

Bishop Museum
1525 Bernice St.
Honolulu, Hawai'i 96817 (808) 847-3511
* Pacific, natural and cultural history.
* planetarium

Out-of-State Organizations

International Mountain Bike Association IMBA
PO Box 7578
Boulder, CO. 80306 (303) 545-9011
* mountain bike advocates

National Off-Road Bicycling Association NORBA
One Olympic Plaza
Colorado springs, CO. 80909 (719) 578-4717
* race directors
* insured events
* race licenses

League of American Wheelman LAW
6707 Whitestone Road #209
Baltimore, MD. 21207

Accommodations

Hotels
Outrigger Hotels (800) 462-6262
Sheraton Hotels (800) 325-3535
Hilton Hotels (800) 445-8667
Best Western (800) 528-1234

Youth Hostels/Bed and Breakfasts
Hawai'i Backpackers (808) 638-7838 Hale'iwa
Island Hostel (808) 942-8748 Waikiki
Ali'i Bluffs Bed & Breakfast (808) 235-1124 Kaneohe
Breck'n Packers Hawaiian Hostel (808) 638-7873 Sunset Beach
Hawaiian Seaside Hostel (808) 924-3306 Waikiki
Waikiki Hostel & Hotel (808) 924-2636 Waikiki

Foods

Local favorites
Grace's - plate lunches
Masa's - plate lunches
Ono Hawaiian food - Hawaiian food
Ft. Ruger Market - Hawaiian food
Big Kahuna's - sandwiches/pizza
Bueno Nalo - Mexican food
El Burrito - Mexican food
Irifune - Japanese food
Down to Earth - health and vegetarian foods
Leonard's Bakery - malasadas, pao doce, sweet bread
Kaneohe Bakery - buttermilk crullers
Bubbies Ice Cream - gourmet ice cream
Matsumoto's Shaved Ice - island snow cones

References

HBL's *Spoke-n-Words* monthly bicycle publication
IMBA's *Trail Development and Construction for mountain biking* and the *Educational Package.*
A nature walk to Ka'ena Point - by Edward Arrigoni
Hawai'i's Birds - by Hawai'i Audubon Society
Enjoying birds in Hawaii - by H. Douglas Pratt
What bit me? - by Gordon Nishida and Joann Tenorio
The essential guide to O'ahu - by Ruth Girnani-Smith
DLNR's *Trail Inventory*
Gill, Lorin. - naturalist
The essential guide to O'ahu - Gurnani-Smith, Ruth. 1988
Atlas of Hawai'i - Dept. of Geography University of Hawai'i. 1983
Bryan's Sectional Maps of O'ahu - EMIC Graphics, 1995
Sites of O'ahu - Sterling, Elspeth. Summers, Catherine. 1978.

Glossary

'Aina - Land.
Aloha - Hello, love, goodbye.
Boardwalk - Wooden or synthetic planks tied together to create a walkway that prevents the biker/hiker from touching the ground below.
Bunny hop - With both feet on pedals and grasping firmly to handle bars, able to "get air" or elevate your entire bike while riding without a jump source.
Dab - Touching the ground or any solid object with your arms, body or feet to regain balance when riding.
Dismount - To get off the bike. Dismount to safely pass a difficult or unridable section of trail.
Drop-off - A ledge or area of trail with significant variation of

height. Small cliff.

Elevation range: This is the estimated elevation of the trail area.

'Ewa - Direction: towards 'Ewa Beach.

4WD - Four wheel drive (may pertain to dirt road).

Granny gear - the lowest gear on your bike. Enabling easier pedaling on steep uphills.

Kapu - Keep out.

KPSTS - Ka'ena Point Satellite Tracking Station.

Mahalo - Thank you.

Makai - Direction: towards the ocean.

Mauka - Direction: towards the mountain.

Na Ala Hele - "Trails To Go On," a. State trail and access program

NARS - Natural Area Reserves System. A native species protection area.

Off-camber: A section of trail that is excessively uneven, usually angled towards a cliff.

Single track - A narrow dirt path cut through raw vegetation consisting of uneven terrain and natural obstacles.

Skid - The action of a non-rotating tire, when bike is moving forward.

Switchback - A trail that zig-zags up or down a mountainside.

Trails - Meaning single track or 4WD road. Unpaved road.

Trials - A style of riding that incorporates the negotiation of difficult and technical terrain without "dabbing".

Waterbars - Cut logs that are strategically placed diagonally across the trail, partially imbedded into the soil. This helps control erosion by rerouting water run off.

Wheelie - Pedaling or pulling up hard enough to lift the front wheel off the ground while riding.

Whoop-D-Doo's - A series of large dips in the road.

What others are saying about *Mauka Trails of Hawai'i*;

"As a result of trail damage and concern over public safety, the State must consider regulation of mountain bikes on various single track trails. However, both hikers and mountain bikers agree that greater awareness of how fragile our trails in Hawai"i are, is a vital link to solving the problems associated with multiple-use of trails.

Mauka Trails of Hawai'i is a very comprehensive guide to appropriate and conscientious mountain biking. It is encouraging to see attention given to such topics as trail maintenance and trail riding etiquette. If this message is taken to heart, the reader may actually become part of the solution and not the problem."

Curt A. Cottrell - Na Ala Hele trail and access program
State Division of Forestry and Wildlife

"As a hiker and outdoorsperson, I applaud John's efforts to expose Hawai'i's beauty by promoting its trail network. Responsible riders can see more of the State's beauty in less time with little or no impact to the trails. Done properly, riders can reduce conflicts between the different user groups."

John W. Farrar - Official
National Off-Road Bicycling Association NORBA

About the Author

John Alford is an avid mountain biker and hiker in Hawai'i. He works full time as an Emergency Medical Technician with a local ambulance service. Born and raised in Hawai'i, John has spent most of his life on the beach and in the mountains enjoying Hawai'i's natural environment. He raced in local mountain bike competitions from 1989-91 where he sometimes placed first in the intermediate, sport and expert divisions. Although he has dropped out of the competitive scene, John still rides for recreation and enjoyment and volunteers to help maintain state trails.

Through the distribution of *Mauka Trails of Hawai'i*, John hopes to convince mountain bikers that they need to preserve our natural resources and minimize their impact on our precious and fragile ecosystems. John's goal is to promote mountain biking in Hawai'i with a firm emphasis on safety and etiquette. John hopes that readers will be supportive of these efforts by convincing others to ride responsibly and respect the environment. This way, future generations may enjoy the mauka trails that we ride today.

Notes:

Order Form

If this book is unavailable in your area, you may obtain more copies by mail order. Simply fill out the order form below and mail it with the appropriate payment.

Name_____

Address_____

City_____ State_____ Zip Code_____

Qty.	Book Title	$12.95 ea	Shipping	Total

Add 4% sales tax, if purchasing from Hawai'i.
Also, add $2.00 shipping and handling per book.

Please make check or money order payable to:

'Ohana Publishing
P.O. Box 240170
Honolulu, Hawai'i 96824-0170
email: mtnbike@aloha.net

Allow 4 to 6 weeks for delivery.

Coming in 1996: *The Mountain Biker's Guide to the Hawaiian Islands*